# ONE MORE TIME!

To
Kristen
"
"
Musically yours,
Jae Sinclair
10/28/09

# ONE MORE TIME!

## The Dal Richards Story

Dal Richards

*with*

Jim Taylor

HARBOUR PUBLISHING

Harbour Publishing Co. Ltd.
P.O. Box 219, Madeira Park, BC, V0N 2H0
**www.harbourpublishing.com**

All photos from the collection of Dal Richards unless otherwise noted. Additional photograph captions: Page 5—*Remembrance Day concert at the Orpheum Theatre in Vancouver, 2003.* Page 6—*One of the first rules of the band business is that you go where the gigs are. So, why not perch atop a small boat to entertain at the* Vancouver Sun's *free salmon derby? The fishermen seemed to enjoy it. The fish had no comment.*

Cover photograph by Dave Roels
Edited by Ian Whitelaw
Cover design by Anna Comfort
Text design by Martin Nichols
Printed and bound in Canada

Harbour Publishing acknowledges financial support from the Government of Canada through the Book Publishing Industry Development Program and the Canada Council for the Arts, and from the Province of British Columbia through the BC Arts Council and the Book Publishing Tax Credit.

**Library and Archives Canada Cataloguing in Publication**

Richards, Dal, 1918–

   One more time! : the Dal Richards story / by Dal Richards with Jim Taylor.
   ISBN 978-1-55017-492-2


1. Richards, Dal, 1918-. 2. Jazz musicians—Canada—Biography. I. Taylor, Jim, 1937– II. Title.

ML422.R513A3 2009      781.65092      C2009-904053-0

For Muriel, who keeps
me tap dancing…

# Contents

# ACKNOWLEDGEMENTS

Thanking every individual who helped make my life as memorable as it has been would take another book—so instead I want to thank everyone who ever played with my band, sang with my band, danced to my band…or just enjoyed the music.

I'd also like to thank everyone who graciously agreed to be interviewed for the book; whether your name is mentioned or not, your input was integral. To my friends in music, the media, the hotel industry and tourism, at Variety, BCIT and particularly to Paul and Judy and Steve at the Sound Kitchen; to Dal's gals who organized my 90th birthday and continue as friends and advisors today, and to my family, especially to Muriel, who agonized over every word almost as much as I did, thank you.

This is not a biography…but a memoir of my professional life in the city that I have lived, loved and worked in for the past ninety-plus years. Thanks to Jim Taylor for encouraging me to put it all down on paper.

# FOREWORD...

So here I am, standing backstage in the magnificent Orpheum Theatre, wondering what I'm doing here and whether I can pull it off.

I'm ninety years old, for God's sake! Ninety-year-olds don't sell out theatres, not even if it *is* their birthday party. Funerals, maybe, but big band concerts? No way. But they've told me all 2,700 seats are filled, no freebees, and we could have sold more. *Somebody* must think we can do it.

Still...

In a minute, pianist Diane Lines is going to play the arpeggio into my theme song, *The Hour of Parting*, and I'm going to walk out there to conduct my orchestra, introduce the guest talent, sing a few songs ("A ninety-year-old *crooner?* Does this guy have guts, or what?") and basically be onstage for the whole show.

I'm tense, but not nervous. This isn't my first pressure performance or even my first big birthday party. We threw one on my eightieth, a dinner for about 200 people at my old stomping grounds, the Hotel Vancouver's Panorama Roof, and sold out the Massey Theatre for my eighty-fifth. Last night's dinner dance in the BC Ballroom of the Fairmont Hotel Vancouver on my actual birthday was a smash, the souvenir program written and edited by Ann Collette an instant collector's item. So I'm one day into my ninety-first year. Big deal.

But...what if I blow it?

What if I forget something, get the order wrong? Sure, Tony Bennett sings about twenty-five songs in his shows without cheat sheets or teleprompters, which is amazing, but he's only eighty-two! Shows have to be memorized. What comes first? What's next? What if I *miss* something? All that talent out there and the guest of honour blows it? What if…

Wait a minute…

The talent. No matter what happens, the talent will save us. We have a dynamite show. I know this because we've just come off a hot three-hour band rehearsal. We have bluesman Jim Byrnes. We have Michael Kaeshammer, Canada's hottest pianist. We have the Chor Leoni men's chorus. We have two of the country's finest classical pianists from University of British Columbia—my nephew, Corey Hamm, and Robert Silverman—combining for a twin-piano *Happy Birthday* concerto that's guaranteed to bring down the house. We have our old friends Red Robinson and Peter Legge as MCs and the world's only billionaire trumpet player, Jimmy Pattison, to play his own version of *Happy Birthday*.

We're bullet-proof. Which leaves only one question: How will the crowd react when I go onstage?

Okay, it's a birthday party and the place is full, but who's out there? The sixty-plus crowd who remember the New Year's Eve dances at the Roof? The seventy-plusers who danced to my band at the Palomar and quenched their thirst with swigs from brown-bag bottles? The radio listeners who'd heard our broadcasts from the Roof so often they could recite the intro—*"It's Saturday night, and the CBC presents the music of Dal Richards and his orchestra from the Panorama Roof, high atop the Hotel Vancouver overlooking the twinkling harbour lights of Canada's gateway to the Pacific…"?* The crowd that comes to our Pacific National Exhibition shows year after year because the music never dies and never will?

There's only one way to find out. I look over at stage manager Jane Heyman. She nods to me, I nod to Diane, she begins her arpeggio, and I make the walk I've made thousands of times in theatres, clubs, hotels and dance halls of every description for better than seventy years.

The welcome is thunderous. People are rising from their seats to applaud, all ages, twenties on up. Maybe it's anticipation of the show to come. In a sense, maybe it's a thank you for the music through the years. No matter. It's warm, wonderful, gratifying and humbling all at the same time.

When my time comes, I think, this is how I want to go: a full house, leading my band, sharing the music with people who love it, too. What better way to say goodbye?

But not yet. Not when I'm still on top of my game with the gigs coming in and the young talent coming up, kids who haven't heard the stories of how it was when the dance pavilions were full and the music came on wax and radio, not internet and iPods.

I turn to the band. We break into *In the Mood* and we're off. I'm doing what I've done all my life. The crowd is turned on—I am, too—and the show is going to be great. I'm home.

# CHAPTER 1

# Prelude

*"You want to make $6 a night*
*the rest of your life?"*

Harmon Leslie Richards, 1938.

A sk anyone: at some point or points in our lives things happen that serve as inspiration, trigger, encouragement or just plain kick in the butt to get you moving. Before I was ten years old I had two: a crystal set and a slingshot. Oh—and a missing left eye. Take either away or replace the eye and this might be a different story, or maybe no story at all.

My crystal set wouldn't look like much to today's kids, all seemingly born with a wire coming from one ear and connected to a gizmo the size of a cigarette lighter that holds songs by the thousands. But to a seven-year-old kid dangling a long wire out the window as an antenna, poking a cat's whisker wire into a chunk of galena crystal and moving it around until faint sounds came through the static in his earphones, it was magic.

Yes, we had a radio in the living room—it was 1927!— that could pick up all the local radio stations and even some from out of town. The guy who ran the garage near our house hooked speakers to his radio and put them outside so people could listen to the Jack Dempsey–Gene Tunney heavyweight championship fight all the way from Soldier's Field in Chicago, the famous "long count" bout. Radio wasn't that much of a novelty.

But this was *mine*. I'd built it, just like a lot of my friends had built theirs. And every Saturday night, once I got the cat's whisker in just the right spot on the crystal, I could pick up stations from Cincinnati to Mexico City and listen to CKWX carrying—via its penthouse studio atop the newly opened Hotel Georgia—a *live* broadcast from the Belmont Hotel Cabaret featuring the music of Les Crane and his Canadians and chanteuse Dolly Goldberg, who sang her signature song on every broadcast, *I Left My Sugar Standing in the Rain (and He Melted Away)*, which was also one of the early recordings of a promising young crooner named Bing Crosby with Paul Whiteman's Rhythm Boys. (The Belmont Hotel later became the Comfort Inn, where Michael Bublé worked periodically in the Babalu Lounge early in his career.)

Nine years old, and I was already hooked on big bands. And why not? Hadn't I already seen—well, sort of—live bands? My family had a camp at Boundary Bay on the Canadian side of the border, about a half-mile walk across to the US side to visit Whalen's General Store and, more importantly, a place called the Water's Summer Dance Pavilion, where my cousin, Henry Herlihy, who was working his way through university playing saxophone with assorted groups, was in a five-piece band called the Syncopaters, whose slogan was "Five men who can really heat your doggies." We'd stand on tiptoe outside the pavilion peering through the louvred windows, watching the dancers and listening to the band while we munched popcorn. And one night—who could ever forget it?—there was an *imported band*: Jay Curtis and his nine-piece orchestra *including* a girl singer, who'd been brought in all the way from Bellingham! *Wow!*

*Go ahead, say it: "Aw, wasn't he cute?" Given my activity and the shutter speeds of the day, the biggest problem likely was making me hold still long enough for the shot to register.*

As for the slingshot, well, maybe Somebody was telling me you don't shoot stones at birds.

In those days the slingshot was as much a part of small boys' lives as comic books and the cigarette packs you put in your bicycle spokes to make it sound like a motorcycle. You kept it in your pocket out of sight during school hours because you weren't supposed to have one. After school or during the summer you shot at targets, tin cans, telephone poles and, okay, birds.

I was coming home from David Lloyd George Elementary School in Vancouver's Marpole district where I grew up. My house fronted on a park, and there was a bush area about a quarter-block square. Three or four of us were going into the bush in pursuit of feathered targets. I was the last to go in. In fact, I'd already spied a bird from the sidewalk and let fly, so I went tearing down the walk, slingshot in hand, to confirm my suspicion that I'd felled it.

I tripped. One prong of the slingshot hit the ridge over my right eye, the other prong pierced my left. I was gushing blood. Still, no one realized how serious it was. Home was a hundred yards away so I ran for it. Even then, I was careful to run past the front door and down the long driveway at the side of the house so I could go in through the kitchen and not get the front room all bloody.

Mom called Dr. Andrew Lowrie, they put me in the back seat of the '27 Nash and off we went to Vancouver General Hospital, where the nurse took one look at my mud-streaked runners, peeled them off and washed my feet before they put me in the hospital bed. I was humiliated.

Mother was mortified and frightened. I guess I was the only one who didn't realize that I was in deep, life-changing trouble.

Put yourself in my position: You're nine years old. You can look out the window to the park across the street where your friends are playing and having all sorts of fun. But not you. You're in a room kept dark because that was the treatment in those days: keep the room dark and let the good eye adjust and carry the extra load left by the one you removed with your slingshot. Every day lasts forever and you don't know when, or if, you'll be sprung.

I fell into a deep depression. I had to know where my mother was every minute. I had to talk to her because if I couldn't do that it might mean I was alone. Being alone in the dark was frightening.

Wise old Dr. Lowrie saw it happening, and had an idea. He knew my mother played piano, and sang and acted with a Marpole theatre group that put on shows in the local Oddfellows Hall. "You're musically inclined," he told her. "Maybe Dallas has inherited some of it. Why not send him to a music teacher who could give him lessons with some kind of instrument and see? At the very least it will give him a focus, something to occupy his mind."

Well, my cousin, Betty Hoffmeister played French horn in an outfit called the National Juvenile Band in downtown Vancouver. I guess my folks thought it was worth a shot. Off we went to the band hall. But what instrument was I supposed to try? The decision was taken out of my hands. The two band masters—one for brass, one for reeds—had a simple test. "Purse your lips like this," they told would-be brass players. "Blow into this horn, and see if you can make a sound."

I couldn't.

"Well, let's try one of the reed instruments. See if that's any better."

Just like that, I was a one-eyed clarinet player.

I've wondered from time to time how things would have turned out if my parents had rejected Dr. Lowrie's suggestion. My father, Harmon Leslie "Les" Richards, had started out as a farmer in Agassiz, BC, moved to Vancouver and got on as an apprentice blacksmith in a shop across from the Eburne sawmill. When the owner retired, Dad bought the place, closed it in the early '30s and built a machine shop he ran until he retired some time in the '70s. When I was in high school I worked summers in the shop, some on the lathe but mostly on the anvil where my dad made what were called cold shuts and log dogs—a hook twice the size of my hand. When the logs came off the boom up from the river and into the sawmill these log dogs grabbed them and pulled them up on a chain. When the chain broke, rather than shut down the mill, they inserted a cold shut, a link with a hole in it and a prong that went into the hole. I pounded them out with a fifteen-pound sledge.

Stereotypically, maybe not the type of profession where a guy would be sending his one-eyed kid off to music lessons. But he was a strange duck, my father. In his school days pupils in the first eight grades were in one room. He memorized all the stuff the Grade 8s were taking while he was taking Grade 1. He was like a sponge. As an adult,

*The hard-working blacksmith and the sophisticated lady may have seemed an unlikely couple, but Dad wooed and won her and it worked out just fine. My parents, Olive Ellen Hoffmeister and Harmon Leslie Richards.*

*Swapping memories with brother Mel and sister Dorothy, 1987. My band travels kept me on the road a lot, but we still had a lot of them to treasure.*

particularly after a drink or two on a Saturday night, he could recite Shakespeare, Tennyson, Robert Service and other classic writers almost endlessly.

To me and my two younger siblings—Dorothy, four years younger, and Mel, two years younger than Dorothy—

there was a mystery about Dad we've often discussed as adults: how in the world did our blacksmith father ever meet, let alone woo and win, the sophisticated Olive Ellen Hoffmeister—niece of Second World War hero, Maj.-Gen. Bert Hoffmeister—who lived in the big house in the exclusive downtown residential area in Vancouver. But woo and win her he did, and took her off to Marpole where they raised three kids.

One thing we did know about my father: he was a hard man to fool.

As a kid I guess I was a bit of a hustler, particularly when it came to getting out of chores. I had one of the few bicycles in the neighbourhood and used to make deals with the other kids. They'd get, say, three rides around the block on my bike, and as payment they'd mow our lawn. Come to think of it, maybe I inherited the hustler gene from my father. Consider the episode of the sawdust.

Our house on West 73rd Street had a two-car garage at the back of the lot. The driveway ran beside the house. We had a sawdust burner in the basement, and one of my chores as I went through high school was to shovel the weekly delivered sawdust through the basement window next to the driveway and into the bin below. Knowing that I'd want to use the car for a date on Friday night with my sweetie, Joan McLaren, father had the sawdust delivered on Friday morning and dropped in a pile in the driveway next to the window. It had to be shovelled into the basement or I couldn't get the car down the driveway. I'd bribe Mel to get him to help me get the pile low enough so I could drive the car over it.

*Had anyone been keeping score I'd have lost dating points here (look who's carrying the books) but my Magee High School sweetie, Joan McLaren, and I remain good friends to this day.*

From the start, I liked the music lessons. Who knew, if Les Crane could have a band and play on the radio, maybe some day I could, too. But learning was an arduous process. I began weekly lessons with band master William Hoskins-Sara, who came out of London's famous Kneller Hall, home of the Royal Military School of Music. The studio was across from the old Spencer's store downtown, a No. 17 streetcar ride from Marpole. Right after school a couple of days a week I'd run for the streetcar. Because I'd missed so many classes recovering from the eye injury, they'd failed me in Grade 4, then made up for it a year later by skipping me from Grade 4 to Grade 6. Getting into mischief, as I did from time to time, meant after-school clean-the-erasers duty, which meant I'd miss the streetcar and the day's lesson. Thank goodness for a teacher named Lloyd Magar, a violinist who took pity on another aspiring musician. If the erasers clashed with lesson days, he'd say "Go catch the streetcar." Never did find out who did the erasers those days. Maybe it was Mr. Magar.

The lessons progressed. I reached a certain level of proficiency. Then, when I was fifteen, we heard about a man named Arthur Delamont who had organized a hopeful new venture called the Kitsilano Boys Band. Two things about that band hit me: (a) It wasn't restricted to that school. Delamont was grabbing the best young musicians on the Lower Mainland; (b) That band was going to be making a trip to play at the 1933 World's Fair in *Chicago*!

Three of us—Harry Bigsby, Jack Bensted and I, all of us clarinetists—decided that was for us and headed for Kits to audition. We all made it. We would play at the World's Fair. It couldn't get any better than that. And then it did.

To understand how it all came about you need to understand a little about Arthur W. Delamont—aka "Mr. D"—and the drive that, when it came to his band, made "impossible" a four-letter word.

Born in Hereford, England, in 1892 and raised in the teachings of the Salvation Army, he learned to play cornet in one of its bands, a gig that lasted until he discovered motorcycles and dance music.

He settled in Vancouver in 1928, working as a sideman trumpet player in the theatre bands that accompanied the various acts on stage. But with Busby Berkley's fifty girls dancing atop a dozen pianos up on movie screens and the Great Depression looming he saw the handwriting on the wall: Vaudeville couldn't last. With a living to be made he conceived the idea of the youth band. With, say, fifty members paying, say, 25 cents a rehearsal and $1.00 for private lessons, he should be able to make a living at a time when out-of-work orchestra musicians were playing on street corners over the Christmas season, and scrambling over who got the best corners.

With Delamont, to think was to act. He made a deal with the School Board to use the basement of the General Gordon School as a practice facility for the first of his many bands, which in the early years was named after the school. Through the years he organized other school bands in Point Grey, North and West Vancouver and the 111th Air Cadet Squadron, but that first band—now known as the Vancouver Kitsilano Boys Band—was his passion, so much so, as one Vancouver columnist wrote years later, "when Arthur Delamont died in 1992 at age ninety, the band died with him. He had not groomed a successor. He had not wanted his band to go on without him…"

As the band started winning things, word got around. The Kits band *travelled*—to Toronto to compete at the CNE, to Victoria, once on the midnight sailing of a CPR Princess ship! We had a stateroom! How glamorous could it get? If you could play, the Kits band was the place to be. Mr. D skimmed the cream from school bands in the area. It was as though he knew from the start that the band would be special and would leave its mark on the Canadian music scene. In his wildest dreams even Mr. D couldn't have imagined that six graduates of the Kits band—architect Bing Thom, financier Jimmy Pattison, Bill Millerd of the Vancouver Arts Club Theatre, musician Ron Collier (who worked with Duke Ellington), philanthropist and businessman Dr. Donald Rix and a band leader named Dal Richards, as well as Mr. D himself—would some day receive the Order of Canada. But when it came to his band he was never shy about setting the bar high.

Take, for example, that first trip to the World's Fair competition in Chicago, where we'd be competing against the greatest school bands in the USA. We knew in our

*Arthur Delamont had no doubt that his Kitsilano Boys Band would win the high school band competition at the Chicago World's Fair in 1933, even if our opposition would include the best bands in the US. He told us so and, to our utter surprise, he was right.*

hearts we didn't have a chance of winning, but just before the competition I approached Mr. D. "Just for the sake of argument," I asked. "What if we win something here? What then."

"Not 'if'," he said. "Don't worry about that. We'll win."

"Well, then," I pressed on. "What's next?"

"Next year," he said calmly, "we'll go to the Old Country."

Think about that for a second. It was 1933. You didn't casually go *anywhere*. Just getting to Chicago had been no small feat. We went by train and earned our keep playing in stops along the way: Kamloops, Revelstoke, Calgary, Regina, Winnipeg, Minneapolis and then on to Chicago, where we did concerts on the fair grounds before the competition began and stayed at the Lexington Hotel, best known for being Al Capone's hangout in Prohibition days. Saying "We'll go to the Old Country" was like saying "We'll go to the moon."

"Don't worry about it," he said. "We'll win this, and we'll go."

Okay, fine. But meanwhile, we were in *Chicago*, where every major hotel seemed to have one of the country's big bands, a major miscalculation on the part of the Music Corporation of America, which had booked them all over the city in anticipation of the thousands of tourists flocking in for the fair. But people who'd exhausted themselves seeing the fair weren't interested in hitting the dance floors. They just wanted to put their feet up and rest.

That was when Bensted and I concocted our master plan. Actually we'd stumbled on it by accident in Winnipeg, where we'd played a concert en route to Chicago. We'd found our way to a nightclub called the Cave, where Earle Hill's orchestra was performing. (Three years later, Earle and his orchestra opened the Cave in Vancouver.) Screwing up our courage, we approached the head waiter, explained that we were with a band from Vancouver on the way to compete at the Chicago World's Fair, and asked if he'd please just let us step inside and listen. He said okay, and a whole new world opened.

We wanted to hear all these great bands. At first, we hung around outside the ballroom, just listening. But it occurred to us that what had worked in Winnipeg might also work in Chicago. We started tugging at the sleeves of head waiters or *maîtres d'*, giving them woebegone looks and going into our act:

"Excuse me, sir, but we're a couple of boys from Vancouver here for the band competition and we were wondering if, well, we could sit at one of the tables and, you know, listen to the band for a while?"

It didn't always work, but mostly they said yes, even sent over a couple of coffees once in a while. The ballrooms were only about half full anyway, so why not? And we really did have that woeful look down pat. We went all over the city and heard some of the greatest bands in the land: Ben Bernie and All the Lads ("Yowsa, yowsa!"), Cab Calloway, Clyde McCoy playing *Sugar Blues*, Wayne King (the Waltz King), Art Kassel and his Kassels-in-the-Air Orchestra, Johnny Hamp and his Kentucky Serenaders, Larry Funk and his Band of 1,000 Melodies (bands had names like that in those days) and it cost us *nothing!*

Oh, I almost forgot: the band competition. Mr. D called it. We went out against the field, total unknowns up against bands from all over the US, including the Chicago Boys Band, widely considered to be the best in North America, and we beat them all. Mr. D had worked us hard and it paid off: we scored 225 out of a possible 240 points, which one Chicago critic called "unbelievable!" The hicks from the sticks had pulled it off, to our own and everyone else's surprise—everyone, that is, but Mr. D.

Of course, we still didn't believe there'd be a trip to England. Not even Mr. D could pull that off. Once again, we underestimated him. We were barely home and unpacked before he had us selling band calendars door to door and our parents planning bake sales, whist drives and any other scheme that could put some money in the pot.

*An ocean crossing wasn't going to stop our regular rehearsals. Mr. D saw to that. When the weather allowed, we practised on deck in the invigorating sea air.*

And in 1934, somehow, there we were in London, attending a reception in our honour at Grosvenor House, listening to the High Commissioner for Canada calling us cultural pioneers who would give people a new vision of the Dominion of Canada.

We'd just played our way across Canada to Quebec City to catch a ship to Liverpool—third class, four to a room. Class didn't matter. Bensted and I always found ways to get up to the heady atmosphere of the upper classes, wandering the ship, sneaking into the ballrooms to hear the ship's orchestras.

Direct from the Grosvenor House reception we were taken to the Decca studios to make records. For the first time we were the audience listening to ourselves play. Critics liked the records, too. Our favourite review appeared in one of the magazines devoted to such things. It asked one question: "Can these musicians be *boys?*" We marched through the streets to the Tower of London—instruments in hand, our black capes pinned to one shoulder to show the scarlet lining—and actually played a concert in the empty moat. The capes were a Depression compromise: no one could afford regular band uniforms with their brass buttoned finery, but we had to wear something. Capes looked good and were a whole lot cheaper. We performed thirty-minute shows in and around London as part of the variety theatre presentations—Britain's vaudeville. There was music, adventure, misadventure, and competitions to further hone the skills we'd shown in Chicago, including, as far as Bensted and I were concerned, the two-little-boys-from-Canada dodge.

One of the many hotels and ballrooms featuring big bands was a place called the Kit-Kat Club. We went there, tugged the waiter's sleeve and went into our routine, which we had down pat by then and used shamelessly at every opportunity.

"Sure, boys," he said. "Sit at that table over there and make lots of noise."

Noise? Until then, most of our gate-crashing had come with the understanding that we would make *no* noise.

"Joe Loss is making his first live BBC broadcast tonight," he explained, "and there aren't many people. So, make as much noise as you can."

Well, we could do that. We sat there drinking coffee or whatever soft drinks they put in front of us, applauding enthusiastically as we listened to the orchestra of this man who played forever in London and went on to become a favourite of the Royal Family. (One year later, eighteen-year-old Vera Lynn, who had been singing at working men's clubs since she was seven, made her radio debut with the Loss band. She went on to become a World War II favourite dubbed "The Sweetheart of the Forces," and recorded hits like *White Cliffs of Dover* and *We'll Meet Again*.)

We were too excited to sleep that night. Next morning at breakfast we were telling Mr. Stockwell, the guy in charge of booking our band itinerary, that we'd heard Joe Loss the night before.

"Pretty expensive for you boys, isn't it?" he asked.

"Oh, no!" we said and told him about our gate-crashing gimmick. He must have been impressed. It turned out that he booked the Joe Loss band, and through him we got to listen to other big bands around London, most of them performing under the name of the hotel in which they were playing. We sat in the Savoy and listened to Ambrose (his name was Bert Ambrose, but for promotional purposes he went by his last name); the Dorchester to hear Jack Jackson; the Embassy Club for Lew Stone; Grosvenor House for Sydney Lipton. I was sixteen, Bensted two years older. But there we were, sitting in the ballrooms of some of the best hotels in London listening to the best bands for free, and all because we'd dreamed up the two-Canadian-boys story.

Understand, Bensted and I weren't doing it just for the hell of it. The *music* was the thing. We couldn't get enough of it. And no one could say we lacked nerve.

The band started touring the provinces, doing evening concerts. In Northampton there was a variety theatre featuring the Ambrose Orchestra including, although we didn't know it as we entered the theatre, the great Ted Heath on trombone. Because they did a matinee, we were able to catch it. Back in London we visited the Selmer instrument factory, and who was there testing a new trombone but Ted Heath. Naturally, Dallas Richards had to pluck his sleeve, tell him that we'd heard the Ambrose orchestra in Northampton, we were from Canada and *could he play a chorus for us?* Right there in the factory.

"Oh, no," he said. "I'm just a sessions man."

Yeah, a sessions man who later fronted the best band in England.

Well, I tried.

*Talk about your trip of a lifetime: Four Canadian teenagers, band members (l to r) Harry Bigsby (18), Dal (16), Jack Bensted (18) and Pete Watt (16), off to see the sights of London.*

Northampton, by the way, was memorable for another reason: I almost became a one-eyed and nine-fingered reed player.

The band was short of funds (what else was new) and staying in army barracks. Late one night a bunch of us wandered around looking for food and found the barracks kitchen, a big roll of meat, and a bread slicer. I decided to make sandwiches, turned on the bread slicer, and cut the tip off the forefinger of my left hand.

The old sergeant there wasn't a doctor, but he did a great job bandaging my finger, and just as I was about to faint from the pain he put his mouth on my cheek and sucked as hard as he could. My head cleared, just like that. "Old army trick, lad," he assured me.

Our next stop was Ireland to play the famous Dublin Horse Show, the country's big social event of the summer. By this time I needed my bandage changed. Someone pointed me to a street full of town houses. I picked one at random, did the boy-from-Canada dodge as a solo, and a doctor came right out to take care of me. When I related the incident to the lady of the house where I was billeted and gave the doctor's name she was stunned.

"Why," she gasped, "he's Ireland's most famous surgeon!"

When you're curious and too young to be scared, good things can happen. When we sailed back to Canada we docked in Montreal, where we had a night free before catching the train home. Bensted and I immediately took off for the Normandy Roof at the Mont-Royal Hotel, where a New York saxophonist named Charlie Dornberger was fronting the hotel band. We watched the show, called the *maître d'*, amended our usual plea to two-boys-from-Vancouver, and asked if Mr. Dornberger could come over and say hello.

Dornberger had reason to remember Vancouver. He'd been with the Paul Whiteman band when it showed up to play a ball at the old Hotel Vancouver, and wasn't allowed to perform. In those days the Immigration Department had an agreement with the Musicians' Union: American bands could come in and do stage shows, but not dances, where they'd be replacing local labour. So Whiteman and the band sat around the hotel for a couple of days keeping the bellboys busy delivering bootleg hooch.

As I say, we sat and listened to the band, and then I asked if Mr. Dornberger could come over and say hello. He did.

We asked for his autograph, and he signed it "Musically yours, Charlie Dornberger." It sounded good to me. To this day when I sign autographs or CDs I write "Musically yours, Dal Richards." And I stole it from Charlie in 1934.

What with all this travelling it might be easy to forget that this was a band made up of teenage kids. Put two kids together and mischief can break out. Put fifty or so in a foreign country and the occasional incident was bound to catch Mr. D's attention. Take, for instance, the time the concert was stopped by a high diver.

We played many seaside resorts on our tour of England, a string of them along the south coast, including Eastbourne, Bournemouth, and Shanklin on the Isle of Wight. They all had long entertainment piers and almost all had a dance pavilion at the end. Shanklin's also had a high-dive platform. And I had a bathing suit.

You could go down a ladder off the pier about twenty feet into the water. I decided to dive. The distance was no greater than the dives I'd made at home off the Marpole bridge. So I did, several times. Then someone said "Why dontcha try the high-dive tower?"

I thought about it for a day or two, then climbed up for a look: sixty feet from the top to the dock, twenty more to the English Channel. But I did know how to dive. So I dove, and it was *perfect* except for one small detail. I went down a lot farther than I'd thought, took my time coming up, and forgot about the current. I was about a half-mile down the beach before I got to shore.

Well, that was fun. Over the next few days I did it two or three more times—until the high-diver stormed up to the bandstand, stopped the concert, accosted Mr. D and demanded to know which kid in this %$%## band was climbing up on his tower and diving off? It seemed I'd spoiled his act. He did *his* dives at night in an asbestos suit and a football helmet, sprinkled a little gas on himself and burst into flames as he dove. Now some *kid* was diving off in a bathing suit? How did that make *him* look?

(Funny how those things come back to you. A few months before my ninetieth birthday we were at a pool party in West Vancouver. The pool had a regulation diving board. I kept looking at it and wondering. Finally I walked the board to the edge and did a jack-knife into the water. Daughter Dallas watched that one and gave me a thumbs-up when I surfaced. Perfect! You're only old if you think so.)

*We were playing at a dance pavilion in Shanklin on the Isle of Wight. The pavilion was at the end of an entertainment pier, the water only twenty feet below. Naturally, I had to dive. As it turned out, this one was just a warm-up. See, there was a high-dive tower, and...*

Once we got home it took a while to get back into the regular school routine, but the music was never in any danger of slipping to No. 2 on Bensted's and my personal hit parade. If anything, the hook was set even more firmly.

The Benny Goodman, Xavier Cugat and Kel Murray orchestras shared time on the NBC network's *Saturday Night Dance Party,* a radio show we could pick up live from New York on Seattle's NBC station, KOMO. Benny was playing the so-called "hot" music. Bensted and I hunched over the radio far into the night, soaking it up, not knowing that what we were hearing was the first sound of a musical revolution.

On the strength of that twenty-six-week radio show, Goodman took his band on a cross-country tour, playing the standard stuff the ballroom proprietors insisted was what the public wanted to hear. They laid eggs everywhere. It got so bad that singer Helen Ward, who also played piano, would perform part of the show with only part of the band, the part that remembered waltzes.

Then, on August 21, 1935, they got to the Palomar Ballroom in Los Angeles and were surprised to find the place jammed to the rafters. If they were gonna die this time, they decided, they'd die doing *their* music. They broke into *King Porter Stomp* and the place went nuts. Bensted and I weren't the only ones hooked on that radio show. Apparently thousands of west coast fans loved it, too. Overnight, Benny's band was the hottest thing going.

Bensted and I didn't know that, of course. We were just two kids coming off a great adventure and listening to more of the greatest sounds in the world. Who'd have guessed that one day we'd team up again as he played sax and clarinet for three years in my band at the Panorama Roof?

In terms of hijinks, the diving board episode probably was my benchmark, although when the band returned to London in 1936 there was another that gave it a pretty good run.

The reed section had a free weekend while the brass section competed in a brass band competition at the Crystal Palace, which they won. We had a clarinet player named Bernie Temoin (later a fixture for years with the Toronto Symphony Orchestra as Bernard Temoin) who spoke French. A day off, a guy who spoke French—and Paris just across the Channel? If that wasn't a sign from the heavens, what was?

Bernie, Jimmy Findlay and I (clarinetists all, which a school psychologist might have found interesting if such an animal had been working back then) hopped a Channel ferry and began our investigation of the cultural delights of France by heading for the Lido de Paris, a club renowned for its somewhat risqué musical extravaganzas. To three hormonal teenage boys that translated to one thing: naked ladies! We had such a great time we raced to get the train back to the seaport, got on the wrong one, missed the boat and had to stay overnight in Dieppe in the cheapest accommodation we could find and catch the early boat the next morning. We were eight hours late reporting back to Mr. D, who was not amused. (Jimmy Findlay grew up to be James Findlay, director of special services for the Burnaby School Board. Wonder if he put that Paris trip in his *curriculum vitae?*)

*Ah, Paris! The Eiffel Tower, the Folies Bergère! French loaves! The second trip to Europe, in 1936, was shaping up even better than the first. I sat in a street café, marvelling at my good fortune.*

But I did not return empty handed. During our stay we had fallen in love with French bread, something we'd never seen in Vancouver, especially when slathered with butter and/or jam. Before we left, I bought a loaf with some idea of taking it home for my mother. Upon sober reflection in London I realized that, what with the ocean voyage and the train trip across Canada, the bread wasn't going be in great shape for our kitchen table—but it would still provide a great souvenir of our Parisian excursion. But how to get it home intact? No problem. I went to a small London shop and bought a brush and a can of shellac. By the time we boarded the Empress of Britain it had three coats.

My loaf survived the ocean voyage, despite the fact that it was too big to put in my luggage. As I boarded the train to begin the long cross-country journey—with our usual stops to entertain in city, town and hamlet—I wrestled with the problem of how to keep it safe. We didn't have to change trains. When we stopped to perform, our cars were parked on a siding and hooked to the next train when we moved on, so it was just a matter of finding one safe place for the precious loaf. Finally, I convinced a porter to put it in an unoccupied upper berth. The trip took about ten days, and as the train chugged the Fraser Canyon on the last lap to Vancouver I found the porter and asked him to return the French loaf to my custody. He obligingly opened the berth and found the loaf—broken in half. Somehow it had jammed against something, perhaps when the berth closed. Train trip from Paris to London, trans-Atlantic sea voyage, and snapped in half on a train a few miles from home. I held the two halves of my shellacked souvenir for a moment, and threw them into the Fraser River.

That was my last trip with Mr. D and the band. After much tossing and turning, I decided not to go to San Francisco in '37 to play at the opening of the Golden Gate Bridge. I was on the fringe of the local band business, sitting in with whomever I could whenever I could. In Grade 11 I'd organized an eight-piece band at Magee High School. We played school dances (and got a glowing review in the Prince of Wales school paper after their grad dance) and the local golf clubs for whatever money we could get. Our rule of thumb: try to get $2 per hour per member. Lots of times we settled for $1. As the leader, I'd get $10 a gig. Maybe. I also played Saturday nights with the Johnny Matthews band at the White Rose ballroom on Broadway east of Granville for $6 a night. My parents were disappointed. A weekly salary of $6 wasn't exactly what they had in mind for their high school grad son. But one night, while they were parked outside the ballroom waiting for me and listening, they heard the singer, admitted that he sounded pretty good, and asked who he was. When I told them it was me they may have figured out that I was going to pursue some sort of career in music. Still…"You want to make $6 a night the rest of your life?" Dad asked.

But I had an unquenchable thirst for show biz. One of my fondest childhood memories was the regular Saturday afternoon drive downtown to Woodward's with my parents when I was about ten years old. We'd shop and eat supper in the store, then walk down Hastings Street to Pantages theatre at Hastings and Carrall streets to see top-class

39

vaudeville shows—the golden-throated sopranos, the comics, the acrobats—where, although I didn't know it, Mr. D played trumpet with the orchestra. The excitement of those shows and the glamour of that theatre grabbed me and never let go. I got to where I could tell by the backdrop they were using for the individual acts what sort of act was coming next, which didn't really matter, because I loved them all.

A few years later I caught more vaudeville at the Orpheum, people like the Aristocrats, a three-man acrobatic team whose act included forming a totem pole, the bottom man one Burt Lancaster, who'd go on to become a major movie star. Eddie Peabody, the fabulous banjo picker, packed the theatre to overflowing so, while other acts performed, he went out into the street and played for the crowds that hadn't been able to get in. Another on the circuit was Betty Compson, a '30s movie star whose vaudeville shtick was her impression of Marlene Dietrich, straddling a cane chair, garters peeking out, as Marlene had done in the movie *Blue Angel*, singing *Falling in Love Again*.

The public's appetite for vaudeville and stage shows of all sorts was insatiable in the days before talkies dealt the death blow to vaudeville. Looking at newspaper ads of the era is fascinating. The December 1, 1923, edition of the Vancouver *Daily World* reported that Benny Leonard, "the greatest lightweight [boxing] champion of all time," would appear at the Orpheum "to dance, box and generally entertain." Two weeks later, the same paper had a scoop: "The incomparable Pavlova is coming to Vancouver, for one matinee performance only, at the Orpheum Theatre in early January" with her new Ballet Russe and an ensemble cast of more than sixty.

I wasn't into ballet, but as I grew into my teens I'd go to the Orpheum on Saturday afternoon to see the stage shows. The first started at about 2 p.m. I'd then sit through the movie and shorts to see the second show at about 5 p.m. Seeing the footlights go on and the curtain go up to reveal

*Trips like the two European tours by the Kitsilano Boys Band can forge lifelong friendships, none better than mine with my high school buddy and two-boys-from-Canada partner, Jack Bensted, here comparing notes and memories in 1937.*

the musicians sitting there was such a thrill I could hardly stand it. I was sixteen, and knew that had to be the greatest life imaginable. In my head and heart those matinees made it a certainty: somehow, some way, I had to become an orchestra leader.

Big dreams, those—but a few years later we had a shot at the big time: a chance to put a band in a ballroom at the end of the English Bay pier at the entranceway to Stanley Park for the summer, a spot not unlike the ones we'd played in England with the Kits band. I don't know why we were asked to audition. Maybe someone had heard us at a golf club and figured a really young band would be an attraction. Whatever. This was a totally pro gig and I knew other bands around town were after it. CJOR would do remote broadcasts. We'd be live on radio!

Hearts in our mouths, we auditioned, and got the job. The Dal Richards Orchestra, live from the English Bay pier. The band guys got $6 each for three hours. Being the leader got me fifty percent more, so I pulled in $9. Doesn't sound like much now, but in 1937 it was damned good. For a while, I had a secure job. After that, I didn't know. But I'd found my career.

# Everybody Dance

*"Hey, kid, can you lead a band?"*
Hymie Singer, 1938.

To get a true picture of what life was like on the entertainment scene in the '30s, '40s and early '50s you need to know only one thing: Until 1953 you couldn't buy a drink in a restaurant, a ballroom or a club.

This is not to say that the people in the restaurants, ballrooms and clubs weren't drinking. Of course they were. They just brought the booze in with them and bought the set-ups—mix and ice—from proprietors who just happened to have them there in abundance in case someone happened to develop a sudden craving for a nice, non-alcoholic drink. Teapots were often available, some even containing tea. If a customer happened to have something in his pocket to pour into the teapot to give the brew a tad more bite, was that the proprietor's fault? And if the police should happen to drop in on behalf of forces for good in the community checking to see if anyone was imbibing alcoholic spirits, could they be expected to check every teapot? Of course not.

The laws were silly. Everyone knew they were being flouted, including the policemen who often arrived for their obligatory raids with sirens blazing to give any politician, judge and local bigwig who might happen to have dropped in ample time to drop out or, in the case of the Penthouse, to shift the booze into drawers of tables specifically designed for the purpose. It was much the same at the Roof, minus the sirens. Police had to come through the hotel lobby to get to the elevator to take them up to the ballroom. No matter how quickly they moved they couldn't beat the telephone message from a bellhop or the guy on the front desk to *maître d'* Henry Madson. Henry would signal me, we'd stop what we were playing and break into *Roll Out the Barrel*. The regulars knew what that meant. The booze was stashed and by the time the police arrived, the people who weren't dancing were sipping coffee or soft drinks.

The police weren't stupid. They knew what was going on, and that they couldn't win. For them, it was more a case of being seen *attempting* to enforce the unenforceable. At the Penthouse, a lookout was kept on the roof on nights when it was suspected or tipped that a raid might be coming. At first sign of a squad car he pushed a buzzer that sounded in the club. By the time police got through the door the booze had disappeared into the drawers.

In the late 1950s or early 1960s the Penthouse gave the police an additional reason to be interested in their goings on by bringing in, uh, exotic dancers. Not that the Penthouse was the only club doing this. Vancouver had a reputation up and down the coast for having some of the hottest nightclubs north of San Francisco. Guys looking for a night on the town could dance the night away at one of the ballrooms, then drop in at one of the strip joints to see women with names like Big Fanny Annie and Chesty Morgan. Vancouver was a lot of things. Backward it wasn't. The liquor laws, on the other hand…

In today's wide-open club scene, when downtown establishments can stay open until 3 a.m. and violence has become almost commonplace, it seems hard to imagine times when drinking establishments had one entrance for men and another for ladies with escorts, both going into the same place. But that was the way it was, and only the bootleggers loved it.

Today's musicians are primarily known for live appearances at the local jazz clubs, the CDs or DVDs they cut and the studio work they do—gigs with the TV shows, background for TV commercials. Fifty years ago one rarely cut a record. There weren't independent sound studios you could pop into. The CBC had radio shows that employed musicians at $9 per show, which was a good wage for the time. George Calangis, Harry Pryce, John Emerson, Doug Parker, Dave Robbins, John Avison, Percy Harvey, Ricky Hyslop, Bob Reid, Lance Harrison, Donny Clark and I all benefited from that. But, give or take a funeral, birthday party or bar mitzvah, for musicians—established, struggling or wannabe—the clubs, dance halls and ballrooms were the only places to find work. You made your living on the bandstand and were known by the clubs in which you played. If you did well, you stayed on. Catch on and you could and did stay for a year and longer. Nanaimo-born Charlie Pawlett and his orchestra got a gig at the Commodore Ballroom in 1936 and were the house band through 1939.

Ballrooms and clubs flourished, folded and were reborn under a new name—the Palomar, the Quadra Club, the Arctic Club, Isy's, the Embassy, Alexandra, White Rose, Howden, Trianon and Peter Pan ballrooms, the Alma Academy, the Commodore, the Harlem Nocturne, the Hot Jazz Club, the Mandarin Gardens, the WK Gardens, the Smiling Buddha, the Marco Polo, the Narrows Supper Club at the north end of the Second Narrows Bridge, where Barney Potts' orchestra held court and patrons could hear performers like Ivie Anderson, vocalist with Duke

*Proudly claiming to have "the biggest dance floor in Canada and the only 'sprung floor'," the Commodore was the place to be and to be seen in the '30s. The hard-wood dance floor, built over tires filled with horsehair to give it a distinctive bounce, was a big hit with dancers, here pausing for a photo opportunity.*
Vancouver Public Library, VPL S-70488

Ellington's orchestra. Coffee houses like the Bunkhouse, the Espresso, the Black Spot, the Attic, the Java Jive, the Inquisition, the Ark, the Club 5 and dozens more sprang up and became the places to be—bottle clubs, all of them, complete with cigarette smoke, coffee, pizza and entertainment, some good, some mediocre, all enthusiastic. Sometimes you got to hear people on their way to being famous: Sonny Terry and Brownie McGhee, José Feliciano, Pat Suzuki, all hitting the various towns and their clubs, scrambling for a buck like the rest of us. The easing of the liquor laws in '53 killed off most of the coffee houses, but when the night, the entertainment and the dates were right they could be magical.

Understand this, because it's gotten a little bit lost in the generations and the consumer switch from the ballrooms in front of an orchestra to the living room in front of the TV: Vancouver had, and has, a flourishing jazz scene loaded with talent that would be at home in top bands anywhere. People like Lance Harrison, Fraser MacPherson, Cliff Binyon, Don Dorazio, Gavin Walker, Dave Quarin and Wally Snider on sax; the Chris Gage Trio (Chris on piano, Stan "Cuddles" Johnson on bass, Jimmy Wightman on drums); Jack Townsend, Bob Reid, Bobby Harriet, Bobby Hales, Stew Barnett, Donny Clark, Carse Sneddon, Arnie Chycoski and Stew Barnett on trumpet; Jack Fulton, Dave Robbins and Ian McDougall on trombone; Don Thompson on piano, vibes and bass; Doug Parker, Bud Henderson, Harry Boon, Ralph Grierson, Pat Trudell, Allen Wold and Wilf Wylie on piano; Felix Smalley, Phil Nimmons, Lloyd Arntzen, Wally Snider and Lance Harrison on clarinet;

Oliver Gannon, Ray Norris, Felix Smalley and Ernie Blunt on guitar. To mention them all would require another book. But let me give you two quotes on the quality of local musicians who provided the music in the Cave's salad days, as reported in the *Vancouver Sun* by jazz writer Bob Smith:

> *"Man, they can hear paint dry."*
> —Dizzy Gillespie.

> *"These cats can read around corners."*
> —Paul Gonsalves, tenor saxophonist,
> Duke Ellington orchestra.

And then there was the time that Vic Damone's music was temporarily lost and the Cave band had to play the show cold without benefit of rehearsal. Damone was rightly concerned, but as columnist Jack Wasserman pointed out in the *Vancouver Sun* the next day, he needn't have worried. The Cave band, he said "could read Tchaikovsky's *1812 Overture* off the head of a pin."

From the days when gospel music came out of the chicken shacks in the multi-cultural section of Vancouver's Strathcona area known as Hogan's Alley (gone now, absorbed by Chinatown) through the heydays of the clubs and ballrooms and coffee houses, this city's musicians— and the music they produced—could stand on their own merit.

Today, the city's annual International Jazz Festival is acknowledged to be among the best in the world, and the young people coming out of music schools at Capilano

College and University of BC—several of whom are in my current band—and secondary schools' jazz programs are keeping the standard as high as ever.

But it was into that bottle club, ballroom, post-Depression era that one Dallas Richards, fresh from Magee High School, full of himself and determined to carve a living out of the music biz, took the first of his many bands.

The adventure did not start well. Len Chamberlain had just landed the resident band job at the Trianon Ballroom at Drake and Granville, a fine location in those days because the Yale Hotel beer parlour was across the street. At intermission there'd be a hundred or more people streaming out of the Trianon rushing to get a beer or two down in the twenty minutes before the band came back. I heard that he was short a sax player, and was holding auditions.

I grabbed my sax, jumped aboard a No. 1 streetcar, and headed for the audition. I was terribly nervous. This could be my shot to join an established big band! How nervous? When I jumped off the streetcar, I left my sax beside the seat.

There was only one thing to do. The No. 1 streetcar operated on the Fairview Loop, meaning that sooner or later it would stop there again. I stood there, waiting and hoping. Every time a No. 1 car came by I jumped aboard and rode a block, rushing to the spot where I'd been sitting, hoping my sax was still there. I don't know how many No. 1s I boarded, but eventually I struck gold. There was my sax, still by the seat where I'd left it.

Was that an omen, or what? I rushed to the audition and played Tommy Dorsey's *Getting Sentimental Over You*. To prove my versatility, I also sang a popular song of the day, *Please Be Kind*. It didn't work. I got a "Thank you," but no job.

Oh, I was green. But the years playing and travelling with the Kits band had given me more than my share of confidence, and some lessons had already been learned. For instance, I'd learned in Grade 11 something that would serve me in good stead in later years dealing with promised band gigs and salaries: there was a big difference between money promised and money produced.

One of our English class assignments was to write a poem. The teachers would judge the results and the winner would receive $5, which in those days wasn't hay. I got to work and produced the following:

### A SPRING SONG BY DAL RICHARDS
Come let us sing a song of spring
And gently nodding roses.
A song of brooks and shady nooks
(and softly running noses)
Come let us dance where light romance
Is flung to all the breezes.
(But when spring is bride, the countryside
Is given up to sneezes)

Okay, I was no Longfellow. But the English teacher—whose name, believe it or not, was Miss Language—must have liked it. I won—only to be told that the prize had been changed. It wasn't $5 anymore, it was a free copy of the school annual.

Good lesson: get the money first or the contract in writing.

So much of life is timing. The gig in the ballroom at the end of the pier at English Bay had been fun and a great experience. Now a man named Hymie Singer of the well-known Singer family in Calgary, who had been living in Los Angeles, arrived in Vancouver determined to build a ballroom named after and at least as glitzy as the Palomar in LA. It was a skin-of-the-teeth thing as to whether it would be finished on time. Money was tight. Carpenters would work until the weekend, then threaten not to come back if they didn't get their money. Hymie would do things like pull off his expensive wrist watch, hand it to one of them and say, "Here. This is yours. But bring it back Monday and I'll have your money for you."

But open it did on May 23, 1937, a grand event featuring the Sandy De Santis orchestra. Hymie had plucked Sandy from the Venice Café on Main Street, where he had a five-or-six-piece band that broadcast on CKWX. The next summer Sandy came back from a stay at the Gatineau Club in Hull, Quebec, minus a reed player and invited me to sit in. So I was there, playing sax and clarinet, when Hymie and Sandy had some sort of falling out.

"Hey, kid," Hymie asked, "can you lead a band?"

I'm still not sure why he picked me over one of the more experienced members of the band. I'd been a professional for less than two years. "Sure," I gulped. Just like that, I was the leader of the Palomar band. The next day, Hymie had an ad in the daily newspapers. It read: "Come and hear Canada's Artie Shaw!" (The ad had a major side-effect. My father, noting during my stint as one of Sandy's sidemen that the night work left much of my day free, had a suggestion: why not take a course at the Sprott-Shaw business school at Robson and Howe streets, which was within walking distance of the Palomar? I did, and actually was enjoying it until I saw Hymie's ad. Canada's Artie Shaw? I never even went back for my books.)

Heady days for a twenty-year-old, and for a while there they got even headier. Hymie knew someone in town whose sister was a singer in Los Angeles who wanted to visit and asked if she might be able to find any gigs up here. Her name was Ethel Lang, and she was *spectacular.* In LA, where she'd sung with legendary band leader Ben Pollock— the guy who gave Bennie Goodman his first big break—she was billed as The Blonde Bombshell. One look and you knew why. The boys in the band were slack-jawed. She just blew me away.

Great singer with looks? Naturally, she got the gig. She was eight years older, but we soon became very good friends. We even sang a duet on *Two Sleepy People,* although the irony escaped me at the time. When it was time to head back to LA, she contacted her booker, Jerry Ross, who got her a gig at the Palomar in Seattle en route. I drove her as far as Seattle and we said goodbye. That's one of the things I loved about the band business. It was *so* educational.

When it came my turn to lead the band at the Palomar our regular girl singer, as they were called in those days, was Judy Richards (no relation), a sixteen-year-old whose previous experience was singing on CJOR radio under her real name, Ruby Jones. (Judy went on to become Mart Kenney's featured vocalist and married band member Tony Braden, one of Canada's finest guitarists.) Mr. D's son, Gordon, who played lead trumpet, and I jointly ran the band because even at seventeen or eighteen he was already making an impression in the business. We had endless discussions at the Blue Owl café as we prepared for our opening, mulling over our big problem: what would we use for a theme song? I suggested *The Hour of Parting*, which had been the theme for Earle Burnett's Biltmore Hotel orchestra in Los Angeles before he died in an automobile accident. Trouble was, we couldn't locate a copy of the music. All we could do was hum it. Fortunately, a local pianist named Wilf Wylie, who'd worked in the USA, did know it. He wrote out the music for us and Gordon arranged it for the band. We opened our first show with it, and it's been my theme ever since.

The song has an intriguing history. American composer Gus Kahn was visiting cabarets while on a holiday in Paris in 1930. Everywhere he went, the tango dancers seemed to be dancing to the same beautiful song, but no one seemed to know its name. Intrigued, Kahn tracked down the composer, Russian-born Mischa Spolianski, who said it was called *L'heure bleue*. Kahn asked permission to put English lyrics to it and Spolianski agreed. Irving Berlin loved the song and agreed to publish it, and in 1931 *The Hour of Parting* was released. It's been recorded as a swing number by Stan Kenton, Artie Shaw and Benny Goodman. Our version is, of course, a ballad.

We played for dancing Wednesday, Friday and Saturday nights and broadcast Friday nights on the CBC to Winnipeg until the fall of 1938, when Hymie converted the place to a nightclub, a glitzy showplace that drew frequent appearances by the Ink Spots in the '40s and, later, Frankie Laine and Johnny Ray. In 1952, Hymie booked Louis

Armstrong and the man himself, Duke Ellington. But in the beginning we rehearsed backup music for minor acts from Hollywood, mostly—unicyclists, adagio dancers, acrobats, dog acts and the like, anybody who'd work for $150 a week, which was top dollar in those days.

And we had a chorus line, six girls doing the usual high-kick stuff. One was a seventeen-year-old named Peggy Middleton, clearly ambitious, who kept plucking at Hymie's sleeve or mine to inform us, yet again, that she had a solo act she did to *Top Hat, White Tie and Tails*, and she'd bought the tails, the top hat, the cane and had the music and everything and she was all ready and couldn't we *pu-leeze* give her a chance? Eventually, we did give her a solo as well as her regular routine in the line, and she was good. Very good.

But she didn't stay long. Driven by her ambition, she headed for Hollywood where, as she'd always said she would, she made it big. Her name, by then, was Yvonne DeCarlo. Years later she came to the Roof and, after she and her date were seated, came to the bandstand and asked me to come to her table at intermission to talk over old times and meet her boyfriend.

So I did. Yvonne and I talked for about fifteen minutes. The boyfriend didn't say hello, drop dead or go to hell. He just sat there, scruffy looking in equally scruffy pants and tennis shoes. I didn't get a chance to check him for socks. Normally he'd never have been allowed at the Roof. I guess management was afraid to bar him lest he get mad, buy the hotel and sack everyone. Anyway, that's how I met Howard Hughes.

As anyone who makes his living in the music industry mainstream will tell you, the surest thing of all is that sooner or later, you will get fired. Not always your fault: new management, new approach, new show, see you later. That's how my stay at the Palomar ended in the spring of 1939.

Not to worry. Musicians are nomads, gig to gig or city to city. A band leader named Stan Patton was heading off on a tour of the prairies with his ten-piece orchestra. I caught on as a sax player, we did some rehearsing and away we went, hitting places like Kamloops, Revelstoke, Medicine Hat and finally Edmonton, where we opened at a place called the Tivoli Ballroom in mid-July. It was a Saturday night. At midnight, we left the Tivoli and went out to eat.

As we left the restaurant we heard sirens, saw flames shooting into the sky, and decided to check it out. We walked a few blocks. Familiar-looking blocks. We'd come this way from the Tivoli. You don't suppose…?

Bingo. We got there just in time to watch the Tivoli burn to the ground along with our instruments, our music library, even our jackets. How's that for a really big finale?

We scuffled around Edmonton for two or three weeks with borrowed horns and music, furiously writing arrangements to replace our music library. The Edmonton musicians' local held a couple of benefits. We got a week at Edmonton's Strand Theatre, which helped. Then we landed a job at a summer resort ballroom called Ma-Me-O Beach on Pigeon Lake just outside of Edmonton, "Ma-Me-O" being Cree for "pigeon." (Be a musician: see the world.) We played there five nights a week. The pay was $35 a week,

which wasn't bad for 1939, and an old house to bunk in, for which we were charged a nominal rent.

We finished the season there, heard the declaration of war on the radio, and rode the train home to Vancouver to open at the Alma Academy, a second-floor ballroom at Broadway and Alma, playing there Wednesdays and Saturdays and scrapping around for casual engagements.

And, once again, the timing gods came through for me.

Mart Kenney's orchestra, the Western Gentlemen, was playing at the Panorama Roof atop the Hotel Vancouver. Early in 1940 Mart called Stan, told him he was heading to Toronto for the summer to play the Royal York Hotel, and offered him a job, starting immediately. Stan accepted, and turned his band over to me.

It got even better. About a month later, in early April, I got a call from Stan.

"Mart's leaving earlier than expected, for a six-week tour on the way to Toronto. So the Roof will need a dance band for six weeks. I've put in a word to Mart, he put in a word to management, and you're getting a chance to audition."

We got the job and opened the last week in April, Wednesdays and Saturdays initially, for dinner dancing.

Just like that, the complexion of my life changed. I'd been scuffling all over the city in ballrooms and such, getting gigs where I could. Now I was leading the band at one of the top ballrooms in Vancouver—and, as I've said, in those days you were known by the club where you played.

*Opposite: Ma-Me-O Beach Resort, Pigeon Lake, AB, was a lifesaver for me and the Stan Paton orchestra in 1939—$35 a week and a house to bunk in—after a fire in Edmonton took our music and instruments. That's drummer Tommy McConkey giving me a lift.*

My phone started to ring and I could pick it up without wondering if it was a bill collector. Instead of scrounging for jobs, I was getting offers. Ma-Me-O Beach was a million miles away.

Not that I wasn't always on the hunt myself. In a career as chancy as the band business, where you could be working tonight and fired tomorrow, I operated under the theory that the more jobs I had going the less chance I could be totally unemployed.

In 1944, Vancouver's Parks Board had decided to sponsor a series of free Sunday afternoon band concerts in Malkin Bowl in Stanley Park to go with the Sunday evening shows sponsored by Home Gas and featuring the Harry Pryce Orchestra. Several of us submitted ideas—Harry Pryce, John Emerson and one Dal Richards, then twenty-six.

It seemed a glorious opportunity. The budget was such that we could have a twenty-five-piece orchestra, a string section, singers, the works. My submission was not that far from what the Kits band was doing with classical concerts, except that mine would be called *Concert in Rhythm*, featuring light opera, classics, Broadway show tunes and dance music, too. Darned if the Parks Board didn't sign me up for three concerts that season.

I had listed the classic numbers we'd play. I could borrow the full orchestrations with strings from a friend at Western Music Co. on Seymour Street. But my submission had left out one tiny bit of information: I wasn't sure I knew how to conduct. Oh, Mr. D would occasionally give one or two of us a brief opportunity, and I'd had my own dance bands, but band music was all in one tempo. This would be a full

*Free Sunday afternoon band concerts at Malkin Bowl began in 1944, drawing big crowds and a sea of stylish hats. Three of the concerts that first year marked my debut as a conductor, thanks to a crash course from junior symphony director Gregori Garbovitski.*

orchestra including a string section playing overtures from operas and concert music where I'd have to direct the musicians in and out of tempos and the position of the hands was a signal to them. Hold on!

I went to see Teddy Jamieson, long-time secretary of the musicians' union, and explained my problem.

"Why did you bid?" he asked. Fair question.

"Well," I said, "I had this idea…"

He thought it over.

"I think I've got the guy for you," he said. "Gregori Garbovitski, director of the local junior symphony. He gives piano and violin lessons. Conducting, I don't know. Go see him and find out."

Garbovitski's studio was in one of those office buildings on Hastings Street crammed with one-man operations. I took the music for my planned first concert and explained my problem and how I needed help.

He nodded. Then: "When's your first concert?"

"In three weeks."

"No! No! No!" he exploded. "Go! Go! Go!"

Fortunately, the idea of turning me into a conductor in such a short space of time was so implausible, he saw it as a challenge. He hauled out his schedule and we mapped out as many one-hour sessions as we could in the next three weeks. I think I paid him something like $5 a lesson, which doesn't sound like much now, but in those days...

He'd have his music stand, I'd have mine. He'd sit there playing violin in my direction, always with a cigarette dangling from his lips. I kept waiting for the ashes to fall. It was fascinating. But what I remember most about those sessions, without which I could never have held those concerts, was that he could have said no. He could have brushed me off with a "Don't bother me, kid." But he didn't, and after that intense three-week session I found I was enjoying it and continued the lessons for about a year. That list of people to whom I'll always be grateful? Gregori Garbovitski has a place locked near the top.

# CHAPTER 3

# Duets

*"Don't forget the balcony."*

Ivan Ackery, 1940.

J uliette has a line she likes to use about her years spent singing with my band: "I'm the only singer Dal had that he didn't marry." Not quite true. I had dozens of band singers and married only two.

But I did change her name. Or, at least, shortened it.

It was summer, 1940. I'd been playing at the Roof for a couple of months and I guess we must have been doing pretty well because after all that time rattling around the city playing ballrooms the job offers were coming in. One such call was from Ivan Ackery, manager of the Orpheum Theatre, telling me they now had a Friday night program featuring local bands that cut out some of the shorts between movies—travelogues, the March of Time, comedy skits, that sort of thing. It would start at 8 p.m. and go for about thirty-five minutes, which meant we'd be finished in time to get back to the Roof for the downbeat. Would we be interested? Well, sure.

Ivan was at the rehearsal at the theatre. "Dal," he said, "I notice you haven't got a girl singer. I heard a little girl at the Kitsilano Showboat the other night who is *very* good. She's only thirteen, but…"

No way did I want a thirteen-year-old singing with my band, I told him. Bad for the image. We were a professional band. It would look like kiddies' day at the amateur hour.

"Well, will you at least *listen* to her?"

We already had two male singers. I didn't need another, male or female. But Ivan was giving me a gig. I could listen to this kid as a courtesy, *then* turn him down. So we went to the Showboat and there she was: Juliette Augustina Sysak, singing up a storm. We put her in the show at the Orpheum. It was wartime. She sang *There'll Always Be an England* and brought down the house.

Hmmm…maybe it was time to rethink the female vocalist thing. Juliette would turn fourteen in August and looked much older than she was. Her voice was that of a singer far more mature, and even then she had that reach-out quality that would one day make her a star. Maybe I *could* use a female singer at the Roof.

It wasn't easy. Her parents knew her determination to make singing her career and were very nice. They even invited the band into their home to help celebrate Juliette's fourteenth birthday. But she was still their under-age daughter and the law was still the law. There was only one way we could work it. The contract that stipulated her job and salary would also contain a clause that made one Dal Richards, in effect, her legal guardian whenever she was on hotel property. That left one more thing.

*She started her career at age thirteen, singing with my band at the Panorama Roof, so who better to help me celebrate my tenth anniversary at the Hotel Vancouver than "Canada's pet, Juliette"?* Vancouver Sun photo

Juliette Sysak on a marquee? Too awkward, too hard to remember. She needed a stage name, something catchy. I gave it some thought. "You're not Juliette Sysak any more," I told her. "When you're on stage, you're just Juliette."

I don't know how much difference it made. It was her talent that carried Juliette to the top of the heap in Canada. But "Our pet, Juliette," as she became known on national TV, rolled off the tongue a lot more easily than "Our pet, Juliette Sysak" ever would have.

It worked out really well, once you got past the idea that, in the beginning, the featured vocalist at the Panorama Roof rode her bicycle to rehearsal. The band members took turns picking her up in the evening, driving her to work and then home. There were no incidents. As Juliette said years later, "I didn't know what 'jailbait' meant, but the boys in the band sure did."

Incidentally. Juliette's rendition of *There'll Always Be an England* drew more than local attention once we worked it into her performance with the band. *Downbeat* magazine, the bible for North American musicians, carried this item in its September 1, 1940, edition out of Chicago:

### PATRIOTIC TUNES GET
### BIG PLAY BY CANUCKS

It's taken a world war to make a major change in Canadian song hit standings. Ever since jazz became a major industry in the US, songs have become hits in Canada at the same time or a couple of weeks later. Now Canadians have a song smash that nine out of ten US fans have never heard. It's *There'll Always Be an England*, which to an Englishman is what *God Bless America* is to an American.

## FOURTEEN-YEAR-OLD CHIRPIE

With this nation at war the wise maestri are giving plenty of attention to patriotic tunes. Dal Richards' band, playing a bang up job at the Hotel Vancouver, makes a neat combination of the English song and *God Bless America*, putting both English dancers and American tourists in a happy frame of mind. Richards is using a cute 14-year-old songstress with his band. Real name is Juliette Sysak so Richards calls her plain Juliette. She's got more natural born charm than most chirpers twice her age.

(Another page in that edition of *Downbeat* offers graphic evidence of the state of the big band business in those days: a full-page list, Where the Bands are Playing, gave the location of 796 bands including one "Richards, Dal. Hotel Vancouver, Vancouver BC.)

Juliette stayed with us for just over two years, then sang with other local bands for a couple of years before heading to Toronto to pursue her career. But there was a sequel. One of our many other female vocalists whom I didn't marry was Juliette's sister, Suzanne Sysak, who saw how the single name worked for Juliette and followed suit. Suzanne had a fine career of her own including appearances on *Harmony House*, sponsored by Nabob Foods. Like Juliette, she has a star on the BC Entertainment Hall of Fame's Starwalk on Granville Street.

I carried something else away from that show at the Orpheum, courtesy of Ivan.

The show had worked. I knew that. I was backstage with Ivan, twenty-two years old and all full of myself, thinking "I just played the Orpheum! Louis Armstrong played on

*Orpheum Theatre manager Ivan Ackery was the man who suggested in 1940 that I could use a female vocalist and asked if I would listen to a little girl named Juliette Sysak. Twenty years later, the three of us agreed it had been a great idea.* John Harvey photo

this stage, and Jack Benny, and so many others." I guess I was kind of fishing for a compliment.

"It was a good show, Dal," he said. "But..."

The "but" hung out there ominously for what seemed like a very long time. Then...

"But you forgot the balcony. This theatre has 1,400 seats downstairs. But it also has 1,400 seats in the balcony, and you never once directed any part of your attention to the people up there sitting in them. *Never* forget the balcony."

I didn't. Never again. But it was more than that. Later in life I started thinking about it and realized it could apply to a lot of things. Paying attention when people are speaking. Considering the feelings of your family, appreciating the love they have for you. Don't get so wrapped up in yourself that you don't notice. It's the same with the music. Was I playing what *I* wanted instead of what my audience might want to hear? So I've sort of adopted Ivan's message in daily living, or tried to. Don't forget the balcony.

*Dal Richards and His Orchestra often played early evenings at the Orpheum before running down the street to their nightly gig at the Panorama Roof.*
City of Vancouver Archives CVA 1184-2313

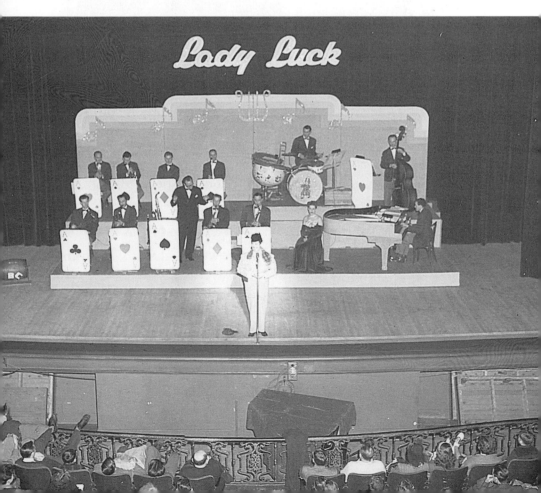

Now, back to Juliette's line and the two singers I married. I lost the second, Lorraine McAllister, to cancer. The first, Beryl Boden, I lost to—well, I guess you could say I lost her to the music.

Beryl was singing at the Cave with Earle Hill's orchestra when I was playing at the Roof. We both lived in Kerrisdale. She was about eighteen and didn't have a car or a licence, so after her show at the Cave she'd walk the half block to the hotel, come up to the Roof, and when we were done I'd drive her home. But for a provincial ruling in 1943, it might have ended there, Beryl with her career, the band with ours. Beryl got her licence, her dad got her a mid-'30s Hupmobile, and she was good to go.

The new legislation, however, turned everything upside down.

It came in the form of an additional tax levy on any facility that offered live entertainment. Bands could still play as usual, but if there was a singer, that would classify as entertainment and thus the establishment would be hit with the tax. Bands weren't entertainment but singing *was?*

Pare away the silliness and what it meant was that I had to let Juliette go and replace her with a singer who could do something else with the band. Beryl could play the piano, which meant she could be a band member who also sang as opposed to Juliette, who was *with* the band but only sang. Ludicrous. But the law was the law. I hired Beryl, who teamed with Bud Henderson on twin pianos. My relationship with Beryl got more serious and we were married March 5, 1945.

Band marriages aren't easy. Crazy hours, crazy lifestyle, two careers, jobs coming and going. We performed and hit the after-hours clubs on a regular basis. Everything centred around our careers because there wasn't time for anything else. I wanted the band to keep getting better and better. Beryl wanted to take her singing career to heights that might never be reached in Vancouver. In hindsight, what happened was inevitable.

One night at the Cave we saw a singing group called Hi, Lo, Jack and The Dame. We got to know them pretty well, and one night after they had returned to New York, Beryl got a call. The Dame wanted to retire. They needed a

*Celebrities were seldom in short supply at Joe Philipponi's Penthouse cabaret, many dropping in after their own shows at the Cave or the Palomar. Here Beryl (far right) and I share a laugh with owner Joe (centre), Donald Mills of the Mills Brothers and an unidentified fan.*

replacement vocalist to appear on the Fred Allen radio show and do gigs around New York. Was Beryl interested?

Of course she was. It could be a big break, and it was. Beryl joined them in '48, stayed about a year, came home for a year, then left for New York for good. By that time we both knew it was over and agreed to divorce. But, my, we'd had some great times.

On an August night in 1945 we joined Art Cameron, then assistant manager (later resident manager) of the Hotel Vancouver, and his wife, Hilda, to attend a show at the Strand Theatre: *Carmen Jones* with an all-black cast—the first we'd ever seen—starring Dorothy Dandridge and featuring jazz drummer Cozy Cole, who was in the pit but on a riser because he was featured soloist from time to time and that way everyone could see him.

The first act curtain came down. We could hear a big commotion backstage and thought they were celebrating someone's birthday. But it was bigger than that. Someone came out and announced that the Japanese had just surrendered. Many in the audience ran out into the streets to see what was going on out there. We stayed to see the rest of the show.

When we left the Strand I immediately went looking for my drinking buddy, Ken "Gussie" Gustafson, because it clearly was party time. But they'd closed the liquor stores. We had no booze, which was a dreadful oversight.

"Wait!" Gussie said. "I've got a bottle of rye in my office."

But the building was locked and he had no front door key, only the one for his office. This was serious. We circled the building in search of access and found one of those fire escapes with the ladder you pulled down, assuming you could reach it, which we couldn't. I climbed up on Gussie's shoulders and pulled it down. Gussie climbed up, searched for an open window, soon emerged triumphantly with a single bottle of rye, and off we went to the WK Gardens in Chinatown to celebrate far into the night.

Beryl went on to a good career in music, remarried, and later launched a second career as a professional golfer. She's written two books, a memoir called *Lucky Star* and a golf instructional called *Play a Round with Beryl Miller.* As a singer, she'd had a hunger to succeed, and did. I couldn't argue with that. I had it myself.

In a way I guess I was responsible for Lorraine coming west to renew her singing career, become my featured vocalist at the Roof and, oh, yes, marry me.

In 1946, Jack Aceman and Charlie Nelson, former operator of the Mandarin Gardens, looked at the slab of concrete covering the vacant lot formerly occupied by the Denman Auditorium and decided it would be a place for an open-air dance pavilion they called the Starlit Gardens. They put up some washrooms, a kind of kitchen and a bandstand. We'd play there Tuesdays and Thursdays, which fitted in nicely around our Wednesday-Friday-Saturday shows at the Roof. Vern McGinnis and his orchestra would play there the nights we were playing the Roof. One night a couple came up to ask me if I'd ever heard of Lorraine McAllister.

Well, of course I'd heard of her. She was well established in the eastern music scene. I'd heard her often on radio broadcasts out of Montreal with the Johnny Holmes orchestra (featuring a couple of guys named Oscar Peterson and Maynard Ferguson) and from the Royal York Hotel in Toronto with the Art Hallman band. She was, I assured them, one fine singer.

It turned out they were her parents, Tom and Mabel. They were going to move to Vancouver, where Tom would open a drug store. Lorraine planned to join them, and they were wondering whether she'd be able to find work. Yes, I assured them, with that voice, she would be okay. And she was. Her first Vancouver gig was at the Commodore with the George Calangis orchestra. Before long she was appearing regularly on CBC radio.

Guy Lombardo sat down with Lorraine and me during our honeymoon stay at New York's Roosevelt Hotel in 1951.

The first time we met I discussed the possibility of her joining the band. The offer went on the back burner, but a couple of years later in 1949 I did need a singer, spoke to her about it again, and she left the Commodore to jump to the Roof with us. We were married in 1951 and she sang with us, off and on, until she became ill in 1983.

Lorraine was almost always in demand as both singer and actress. Home was Vancouver, where our daughter, Dallas, was born in 1951, but she would pop to Toronto for gigs, one a twenty-six-week TV show, *Holiday Ranch*, with Cliff McKay, familiar to Canadians coast to coast as

*Lorraine and I did a lot of TV work together. Here I'm a guest on her network show, Meet Lorraine, in 1958, with the Chris Gage Trio providing the music.*

"Tons of Fun" McKay on the weekdays *Happy Gang* network radio show.

Lorraine's TV career continued in Vancouver with *Meet Lorraine,* a half-hour show with the Chris Gage Trio and a different guest vocalist each week, that debuted in 1958 and ran for two seasons. As far as I know it was the only commercially sponsored show on the CBC starring a girl singer (other than the mighty Juliette, of course). Other TV shows for Lorraine included *Burns Chuckwagon* and *Some of Those Days,* a revolving cast show with Barney Potts as MC and Lance Harrison leading the band. Most of the city's prominent entertainment figures appeared on it at one time or another.

In 1961–62 we were both part of a show called *West Coast,* the first to be produced by the privately owned CHAN-TV. Lorraine did three numbers in each of the half-hour weekly programs, with a guest singer appearing as well. I directed the fifteen-piece orchestra, Barrie Clark hosted and radio man Jack Cullen interviewed stars who were in town appearing at the clubs, mostly the Cave, B stars if you will.

Rehearsals began around noon, which didn't sit well with the stars. It was a long drive to the Burnaby studio, it was at the wrong time of day, it involved a rehearsal and lighting run-through when all they wanted to do was come, do their number and go. Rai Purdy, who'd worked in New York television, was the producer and his wife, Verity, was the choreographer. The comedy teams of Ford and Hines and Rowan and Martin appeared, as did one of the Mills Brothers—Harry, I think—and Frankie Laine. Lots of fun, and good exposure for all of us.

CHAN-TV, the Vancouver outlet of the new CTV network launched in 1960, was soon home for a weekly half-hour variety show called West Coast. I directed the orchestra and Lorraine was the singing hostess. The real trick: getting stars playing the local clubs to show up for noon rehearsals.

Lorraine also found time for regular appearances in *Theatre Under the Stars* productions like *Brigadoon, Desert Song, Hit the Deck, Gentlemen Prefer Blondes* (with Robert Goulet and Fran Gregory, wife of legendary *Vancouver Sun* saloon columnist Jack Wasserman), and *Timber*, written by Vancouver's Dolores Claman. (I don't know how Dolores fared financially with *Timber*, but she did a lot better as composer of the *Hockey Night in Canada* theme in 1968. The tune, regarded by hockey fans as a second national anthem, became one of the longest-running themes in broadcasting history, and when the CBC decided to drop it from the hockey telecasts in 2008, Dolores hit big again by selling it to CTV for use as its hockey theme on TSN.)

*Before Camelot, before heading to Broadway, Robert Goulet spent a summer in Vancouver in a Theatre Under the Stars production of* Gentlemen Prefer Blondes. *His co-star? My wife, the ever-active Lorraine, who ironically had to become a redhead for the role.*

*How does it get any better than this for a band leader? Working at the Panorama Roof in the '50s and getting to croon with a beautiful singer like Lorraine McAllister, who's also Mrs. Dal Richards. Perfect.*

One performance of *Brigadoon* produced a bit of local folklore. Lorraine was three or four months pregnant. Her obstetrician, Dr. Sid Evans, who later delivered Dallas, was in the audience. During one of the more strenuous numbers as one of the dancers hoisted Lorraine and threw her into another's arms, he stood up and yelled, *"Lorraine! You can't DO that!"*

But Lorraine was one determined lady. The way Dallas heard it from her mom, Lorraine was flying home from a gig in Victoria when she started feeling labour pains, which she dismissed as a reaction to a corned beef sandwich. Later that night she woke me, I put her tennis shoes on the wrong feet and rushed her off to St. Paul's Hospital, where Dallas was born later that day, six weeks prematurely, and spent the next month in an incubator. Juliette, back from Toronto for a visit, had been subbing for Lorraine at the Roof, but Lorraine was back on the bandstand long before Dallas was ready to come home. We'd finish the show, then go to the hospital to see our new family member.

Given her seemingly inexhaustible energy, Lorraine didn't limit herself to musicals. The Pantages vaudeville theatre, which opened in 1908 and morphed into assorted burlesque houses (wonderful days those must have been— as the State Theatre it featured a stripper-vaudeville format starring Lois DeFee, "6'4" of loveliness" and a comic named Stinky Mason, who walked onstage backward, waving as if to someone and shouting, "Go fluff your duff!"), reopened in 1946 as the Avon Theatre, doing stage plays featuring names from Hollywood's "B" list. Lorraine caught on as a regular. She appeared in productions like *Of Mice and Men* with Lon Chaney Jr., *Detective Story* with Gene Raymond, and *Mr. Roberts* with Craig Stevens.

And then there was the day she caught some woman wearing her boots. We'd been burglarized a few days earlier. Lorraine was walking downtown when she recognized the boots, a particularly stylish and unique pair she loved that she'd bought in Montreal. She followed the woman home, and then called the police, who recovered the boots and also found most of the stuff that had been stolen.

Ours was a hectic lifestyle, in part because we worked nights, slept in when we could, and crammed our own off-stage entertainment into the middle. In the '50s we had a fascination with Seattle. When we had a couple of days off, we'd jump into a car with our buddies, Mary and Art Jones, right after the show at the Roof, drive straight through to Seattle, get some sleep when we got there, shop all day, go to dinner and then off to see someone like Pat Suzuki at the Colony Club or the Bob Harvey Orchestra in the China Pheasant, grab some more sleep and drive home the next day so we'd be there in time to prepare for a night's work at the Roof.

On another occasion, Lorraine and I decided to drive to Seattle to catch Hildegarde, who was a top name in cabaret entertainment in those days, at the Olympic Hotel. Perry Botkin, Bing Crosby's guitarist and music contractor (the guy who hired all the sidemen for Bing's recordings and

*Following pages: Over Christmas and New Year's, 1952, Lorraine brought a little bit of home to troops in Korea. There never was a more appreciative audience.*

radio shows), whom we'd met when Crosby appeared in Vancouver, decided he'd come along. It worked out pretty well. We sat ringside and Hildegarde, who knew Perry, made a big fuss about us being friends of Bing's.

Remember that time when twenty-year-old Dal drove Ethel Lang down to Seattle after she'd come up from Los Angeles to do a gig at the Palomar? It had far-reaching results. I met her booking agent, Jerry Ross. Some time in the '50s he came to Vancouver to check an act he'd booked into the Cave, dropped up to the Roof, heard Lorraine sing, loved her, and asked if she'd be interested in some club dates in the US. The money was good, so I got another singer to sub for her at the Roof. Lorraine did a few clubs and was very well received. Jerry also had a contract to provide entertainment for the thousands of workers at the Boeing aircraft plant in Everett.

"Dal," he asked, "would you be interested in coming down to do a show with your full band and Lorraine?"

My answer? "Where's the band bus, Jerry?"

It was a great trip. We also did a show at the naval officers' base on Whidbey Island. In both cases the shows were enthusiastically received, and US government hospitality can't be matched.

Lorraine could have worked anywhere. Her warmth and humour made her a favourite in her profession and in life. Upon being named chairwoman of the Marpole women's auxiliary she told a reporter, "I don't have a copy of Robert's *Rules of Order*, so I brought another book: *When in Doubt, Mumble*." The auxiliary's mission was to look after the creature comforts of patients in the George Pearson Hospital.

Our band did a concert there in the Pearson auditorium. When cancer struck and slowly tightened its grip, she kept cookies and candies in her hospital room to ease the tension for friends who came to visit. Her choices to cover the baldness caused by chemotherapy were a succession of the craziest hats she could find.

She died on a Friday—April 27, 1984—at sixty-two. The local daily newspapers, the *Sun* and *Province*, were on strike, but the word spread like wildfire. The next day the employees' strike paper, the *Express*, and every other small paper on the Lower Mainland that was publishing carried an obituary written by Jack Lee. He got it just right in his lead paragraph: *"Tributes today filled the vacuum left by the passing of Lorraine McAllister."* On and off stage, we lost a class act.

CHAPTER 4

# Clubs are Trump

*"By a process of attrition that knocked its competitors out of the race, Vancouver erupted as the café-vaudeville capital of Canada, rivalling and finally outstripping Montreal in the east and San Francisco to the south as one of the few places where the brightest stars of the nightclub era could be glimpsed from behind a post, through a smoke-filled room, over the heads of the $20 tippers at ringside. Only in Las Vegas and Miami Beach, in season, were more super stars available in nightclubs."*

Jack Wasserman, quoted in
*The Greater Vancouver Book* by Chuck Davis.

The big clubs are gone now, but they should not be forgotten any more than should be the men who had the vision and the guts—if not necessarily the cash—to launch them.

Max King rightly deserves credit for ushering in the era of big-name entertainment by gambling $7,500 a week that Lena Horne could fill the Cave in 1946, and later booking people like Sophie Tucker and the Will Mastin Trio, starring the young Sammy Davis Jr. But it was his father, A. Gordon King, who strolled down Hornby Street in 1937, saw a large empty building—on property that had held a livery stable in the late 1800s—and decided that it would be a great place to open a nightclub. Because he already owned a club called the Cave in Winnipeg he looked around for an architect who could give the new place a cave-like feel and hired Frank Holyroyd, who'd designed a dinosaur park in Calgary. Holyroyd moulded sacking and plaster around the support posts, hung stalactites from the ceiling like dripping lava—and Presto! King had his Cave, one of the granddaddies of the Vancouver supper club scene.

*The Cave didn't look like much from the outside in 1948, but it was the showcase for some of the biggest stars on the entertainment scene, and had been since 1946 when owner Max King gambled a staggering $7500 a week to bring Lena Horne to headline there.* City of Vancouver Archives CVA 1184-3470

People who fondly recall the glory days of the Hotel Vancouver's Panorama Roof, of which much more will be written later, will dispute the Cave's claim to the granddaddy title, and it could be argued that the accolade really belongs to the Commodore, which opened as a cabaret, was renamed the Commodore Ballroom in 1969 and was ranked by London's *The Sunday Times* in 1992 at No. 5 on its list of the top ten music venues in North America. (Folklore insists that George Conrad Reifel was persuaded to build the Commodore by his wife, who loved to dance, adored the Crystal Ballroom in the old Hotel Vancouver, and thought it would be nice to have a ballroom of their own.) Another contender would be the Palomar, which opened in 1937 as a ballroom. A *Vancouver Sun* story reported, rather breathlessly, that "several hundred couples were on hand early to dance to the music and enjoy their first sight of this ultra-modern and exceptionally beautiful indoor entertainment palace." It became a nightclub two years later and soon, like the Cave, was one of the places to see live entertainment. The Ink Spots were regulars through the '40s and '50s. Duke Ellington had a five-day stint in 1952.

By the mid-'60s, the trickle of big-name entertainment performing in Vancouver had become a flood. In 1969, over a six-month stretch, Isy's featured the Jimmy Smith Trio, Buddy Rich's second visit, Cannonball and Nat Adderley, and the Oscar Peterson Trio. That same year, over its own six-month run, the Cave headlined Duke Ellington, the Mills Brothers, Ella Fitzgerald, Count Basie and Ray Charles.

*Dal Richards and his orchestra with vocalist Judy Richards (no relation) play on the opening night of the Palomar Ballroom in 1938.*

Wasserman had it right: Vancouver wasn't a backwater entertainment pit stop. But it was a slow process. Isy Walters, who bought the Cave in 1951, obtained BC's first cabaret liquor licence, ran the club until 1958, sold it with the pronouncement that the business was too tough and he needed a rest—and opened his own club, Isy's, on Georgia Street on New Year's Eve that same year. Isy was an entrepreneur. He'd been a candy butcher, as they were called, selling sweets in local theatres, worked in construction at fairgrounds, dealt in scrap metal—one of his truck's regular stops in search of scrap was my dad's machine shop—and operated theatres, but the club scene was his big love, even if he occasionally had to hock his diamond ring to cover the salary of his feature act. A non-drinker himself, he didn't mind if his band drank, but he wouldn't provide the glasses. If they wanted to drink, they had to bring their own glass or find a paper cup.

At the Cave he hired Jack Card, whose own professional career had started there in 1954 as a song-and-dance man with an eight-girl chorus line, to choreograph lavish dance numbers. Jack recalls rehearsals every afternoon for two shows a night, six nights a week. Isy supplied the costumes, the dancing shoes and the net stockings. The shoes cost $10 a pair and lasted six weeks. Because original routines required original material and orchestration, Jack would turn to orchestra leader Bobby Hales, who did several hundred over the years. Jack's costume designer was called in on more than one occasion as the big-name acts would often arrive with stitching gone and hems dragging.

Like Max King, Isy thought big. He booked Tommy and Jimmy Dorsey, Tony Martin, Louis Armstrong and Josephine Baker. But as TV created stay-at-homes, profits and attendance dwindled and the quality of attractions became hit-and-miss. "One week he booked Katherine Dunham and her entire dance troupe," Wasserman reported in the *Vancouver Sun*. "The next week he had Yvette Dare, who had a parrot that took off her clothes. Tommy Dorsey's orchestra was followed by an exotic dancer named Lady Godiva, who stripped to her g-string and panties on the back of a horse."

The big-name acts drew the raves, but it was often the "B" and "C" list types who provided the extra entertainment. Marie "The Body" McDonald, best known for countless cheesecake shots, opened an act in the US and was sent on the road to smooth it out. It was beyond saving. At the Cave she fell down the showgirls' staircase, fired her musical director during the act from the stage, looked up at Card, who was cringing in a corner of the balcony and shouted: "Jack Card! You are a witness to what this man has done to me!"

Then there was the lady pressed into service to work sixteen dogs on stage because her husband, the regular handler, had broken his arm. Things went passably well until a ringsider whistled and threw a piece of meat. The dogs leaped off the stage and ran over, under and around the tables, scattering food in their wake. (Jack Wasserman's wife, singer Fran Gregory, was sitting ringside with Jack Card. Her dress and hair were covered with potatoes, peas and gravy.) And let us not forget the man who balanced a table on his chin and did bird whistles.

But that's always been the thing about the entertainment business. It's chicken today, feathers tomorrow. It takes a special kind of nerve and determination to realize that and hang in anyway. When Ken Stauffer and Bob Mitten ran the Cave through the '60s and into the mid-'70s, the 700-seat club became a favourite spot for big-name performers to break in acts in preparation for Las Vegas. People like Mitzi Gaynor, Juliette Prowse and comic Joey Bishop were regulars. Mitzi, in particular, loved it here, returning year after year, and was loved in return by audiences who packed the place at her every appearance.

I appeared with her once at the Vogue Theatre. My band was to back her up, conducted by her bandleader. Mitzi wanted to introduce me. I suggested we do it as part of the show: she introduces me, we do a couple of soft shoe steps, and I sing *"Hell-o, Mitzi! Well hell-o, Mitzi! It's so nice to have you back where you belong"* to the tune of *Hello, Dolly.*

"Great," said Mitzi, "but let's build it up with a few dance steps."

And that's what we did. There was only one problem. When we finished the dance steps I had to get back into position to sing. I managed, and burst into song:

"Hell-o, Dolly! Well, hell-o, Dolly!"

"Mitzi, Dal," she reminded me. "Mitzi!"

But I recovered. We happened to know that Mitzi had just had a birthday. We played a special "Happy birthday, dear Mitzi." People close to her said the tribute left her close to tears.

And then there was—and is—the Penthouse, now in its sixty-first year of operation, not counting the three years it was closed while a famous court case dragged on in which the founders and owners, brothers Ross, Mickey and Jimmy Filipponi and Joe, the eldest and the family head (whose name was spelled Philipponi after a customs agent spelling error when the family arrived from Italy), were charged with living off the avails of prostitution and assorted other things, a case they finally won on appeal. If you're talking entertainment history in Vancouver, you've got to speak of the Penthouse in all its various forms.

The building, now a garish purple, is only two storeys high. Originally it held a radiator shop in front and a Diamond Cab taxi garage in the rear. In the '40s Joe turned the front into the Eagles Boxing Club for troubled kids by day. At night he'd hold parties in his second-floor apartment,

*Mitzi Gaynor was performing at a fund-raiser at the Vogue, not her usual gig at the Cave, when I was asked to come on stage and surprise her by singing* Happy Birthday.

events that routinely saw so many police visits that when a *Sun* headline read "Joe's Penthouse Raided," Joe said to hell with it, opened a supper club in 1947, and called it the Penthouse.

You might say it caught on. Stars like Sammy Davis Jr., Nat King Cole, the Mills Brothers and Harry Belafonte would hang out there after their own shows at the Cave or Isy's. Errol Flynn dropped in the night before he died. Yes, there were and are strippers, and the early years' tag as a hangout for strippers was no doubt warranted. But so is the other part of the Penthouse mystique, that of a showcase for some of the hottest acts ever to hit town. That's why the club has been named to the BC Entertainment Hall of Fame.

If the big clubs attracted the big acts and the smaller places drew the lesser lights and newcomers testing their acts and their staying power, one other group of establishments must also share the credit for keeping the entertainment business going. In the days before the liquor laws changed, the bootleg joints lubricated them all.

One of the most popular was a place conveniently located across the street from the Penthouse. The joints had no names, of course. They were hardly in a position to advertise. But around town everyone knew about the place run by a black lady who'd also appeared in televised Aunt Jemima pancake mix commercials. It was known— remember the times, now—as Nigger Jean's. When the pleasure-seekers finished dancing in the Spanish Grill at the old Hotel Vancouver, they'd finish off the evening and assorted bootleg spirits at Jean's.

Jean's live-in was a popular piano player named Don Flynn. I played one gig with him while I was at Magee, at the Stanley Park Pavilion when it had a balcony from which the band would perform. We'd play and he would peer down at the crowd, point to assorted women and, in colourful terms, admire their attributes. I was impressed that he even knew who these socialites were.

There were all sorts of bootleg establishments in all sorts of locales—some in restaurants, upstairs, above a Granville Street florist's shop, in residences…there was even one place that featured an elaborate electric train set with tracks that circled the tables. You ordered your drink and it arrived by train. For some customers there was a sort of gee-we're-breaking-the-law thrill to it. Mostly, though, it was the

*Road trip, 1945. Off to Portland for a gig at the Jantzen Beach Ballroom.*

same reaction that made Prohibition unworkable in the US: no one was going to tell people out for a good time that they couldn't drink.

Yes, the big clubs are gone now. Before long there won't be anyone left to remember the Cave, the Palomar, Isy's and the entertainment—great, good, mediocre and not so good—that filled their stages. When the best in the world can be brought into your living room at the flick of a remote, I suppose it was inevitable. Times and tastes change. But they were special times, and we are the poorer for their passing.

# CHAPTER 5

# Star-Gazing

*"I was born in 1983 and I'm never going to see Louis Armstrong or Glenn Miller or Benny Goodman. The fact that I get to live in the same lifetime with Dal and hear him tell stories of those times, that I'm able to share both the past and the present with him, the chance to preserve the nostalgia and talk to someone who was* there—*I never take these things for granted. They're irreplaceable to me."*

Bria Skonberg, trumpet and vocals.

Oscar Blank was panic-stricken. Bing Crosby was in town, had been for three days, and he had yet to set foot in Oscar's Restaurant. The place was "the Home of the Stars!"—everybody knew that. The big names playing the Cave, the Palomar, the Orpheum or any of the other entertainment centres would show up at noon for breakfast. It was tradition, for cripes sake. But *Bing Crosby* was ignoring the place? Or, worse yet, didn't know it existed?

Bing was in town, all right, and he'd brought his entire Philco Radio Time show with him—Marilyn Maxwell, Ray

Milland, Joe Venuti, orchestral contractor and guitarist Perry Botkin, musical director John Scott Trotter—for the sod-turning for the Sunset Memorial Community Centre on September 22, 1948. He'd raised $22,000 in the funding drive by broadcasting his show live from the Vancouver Forum. I supplied the band. We'd rehearsed at the Orpheum. The show itself would be at the Forum.

Bing's Philco show became something of an entertainment landmark. With his encouragement and support it was the first radio show to record with a new technology called audio tape, replacing the large wax discs previously in use. The recorders used were then produced for public sale by the Ampex Corporation, which paved the way for recordings that could now be played, wonder of wonders, in your very own home!

Those tapes became quite a fascination at the CBC studios where the show was "mixed" for broadcast. Some of the music was from the rehearsal at the Orpheum, some from the actual show. And when the show aired, *no one could tell the difference.* How much further could technology go?

I was a semi-regular at Oscar's, located in the Palomar Building at Burrard and Georgia. I'd drop in from time to time and there they'd be: the Mills Brothers, Johnny Ray, Frankie Laine, Sammy Davis Jr.... I got to know a lot of them. Oscar knew my band was backing Bing's show. He got on the phone, almost pleading: was there *anything* I could do to get Bing to drop in? If he didn't, Oscar might never live it down! Home of the Stars! Ha!

Well, I was able to manoeuvre things so Bing and some of the cast went to Oscar's after the show closed. There was only one slight hitch: Oscar was so concerned that things go well that he went into the kitchen and had a few drinks to fortify himself for the occasion.

Actually, he had more than a few. He had enough that we had to all but drag him out of the kitchen. Naturally, Oscar wanted a picture with Bing. Naturally, there was no photographer. I phoned proprietor Harold Lim at the WK Gardens restaurant in Chinatown where there was almost always one hanging around. "Throw him into a cab and get him over to Oscar's," I said. "Fast!"

The guy arrived, Oscar and I arm-in-armed our way over to the table just in case Oscar came down with the staggers. Oscar met Bing and got his picture. Oscar's was still the Home of the Stars!

*It took some doing, but we finally got Bing Crosby to Oscar's restaurant— "The Home of the Stars" for a shot with the nervous and well-fortified owner, Oscar Blank (standing behind Bing and Lorraine).*

I arranged one other visit. Lorraine and I took John Scott Trotter to the Penthouse. He was fascinated. But I couldn't persuade Bing to come indulge in its charms. I suspect he had other plans.

Musicians always had restaurants or beer parlours that were favourites, mostly because the food was cheap, but also because hanging together at one spot put you in a position to hear the gossip about possible steady jobs, one-night stands, auditions or rumours of impending band changes. Rumours, fate and circumstance could change a lot of lives. For instance, consider this conversation between three trumpet players—Ray Smith, Jack Townsend and Stew Barnett—as they sat around the Hotel Georgia beer parlour, all searching for gainful employment.

"I hear Richards is looking for a trumpet player," Townsend says.

"De Santis is supposed to be looking for a guy at the Palomar," says Barnett. "I'll try for that."

Smith had other ideas. "I've got a chance to go to work in a box factory. I think I'll take a look at it."

Good choice. The box factory was MacMillan Bloedel. He got the job, stayed with the company, and went on to become its CEO.

Rumours never were in short supply. There'd always be some entrepreneur with big ideas of forming the next great band. He'd get three or four local musicians, meet us all at, say, the Castle beer parlour and lay out these grandiose plans. Nothing ever came of it, but we kept listening because maybe the next one was the one who'd do it. In the '30s and '40s, when nobody had any money, you lived on cheap food, rumours and hope.

At the Top Hat restaurant on the corner of Smythe and Granville, you could get fruit salad for 25 cents, coffee for a nickel. No booths, only stools, but that fruit salad went a long way. My band and singers hung out a lot after hours at Love's Café, an all-night restaurant in the 700 block of Granville Street, exchanging cracks with an old-school waiter named Albert—apron around his waist and an answer for every wisecrack thrown at him because he'd heard them all. Or we'd trudge up two flights of stairs to the WK Gardens in Chinatown, which in its glory days in the '30s had floor shows and an orchestra but now was down to the restaurant, the dance floor and an old juke box. We'd order a pot of tea, sit four or six to a table, and someone would pull out a mickey and pour it into the teapot before we had our food.

Broke, sure, but oh, they were glorious times. The music was always there, and even if you didn't have a job where you could play it, you could always find a place and an opportunity to listen to some of the greatest sounds in the world. Many of the nickels pumped into the juke box went for *T.D.'s Boogie Woogie*, whose unforgettable driving beat later had some critics suggesting that Tommy Dorsey was actually the father of rock 'n' roll.

In that sense, not much has changed. It's still difficult to make a comfortable living in music in Vancouver. If there are, say, one hundred musicians in the city, twenty-five will be doing fine, but for the rest it's a scramble. Some have their traplines—a series of gigs where they perform every year. Some teach private lessons, some get day jobs, some take their holidays during the PNE so they can play the whole show. It can be unsettling, waiting for that phone to ring, but it's part of the profession.

In today's mega-media marketplace in which the big attractions play the hockey arenas and football stadiums— the only way promoters can hope to generate the money they demand—it's probably difficult to imagine the '30s and '40s in Vancouver, when some of the biggest names in show business were regulars at places like the Cave and might wind up in your kitchen after hours, as Lena Horne wound up in mine.

Lena had made history in her first Vancouver appearance in 1946 when Max King came home from military service to run the Cave and decided it was time to forget about the vaudeville acts that were the entertainment staple under the stewardship of his father, A. Gordon King, and go for something big. He took a deep breath and offered Lena— about the biggest thing in show business at the time—a staggering $7,500 a week to play the Cave.

Max knew it was a gamble. He needn't have worried. The phone started ringing as soon as word got out. A few hours before the first show, Gordon King asked, "How many reservations?"

There were 1,500. The Cave's capacity was 1,100.

"I'm going home," Gordon said.

By showtime the crowd stretched from the Hornby Street entrance up the block to Georgia and along Georgia to the Hotel Georgia. Someone was sent out to nab the club's regulars and sneak them down the lane and in through the back door. I knew the head waiter and had a ringside seat. I was twenty-eight years old. Lena was show-stopping gorgeous. I have never had a bigger thrill than watching that show. It was a triumph, and it opened the door for a stream of big acts that made Vancouver a stop for the next two decades.

Many years later we were the band backing her in another Vancouver appearance. The evening ended with a bunch of people in Lorraine's and my Kerrisdale home, Lena sitting quietly on a stool in the kitchen sipping Scotch as the party swirled around her. Unknown to us, Dallas had awakened and crept down a few stairs to watch the goings-on. Lena made quite an impression on her. The next day, our little girl was sashaying around the house, snapping her gum. Her mother was not impressed.

"Dallas," Lorraine said, "I've told you not to do that."

"Well," replied Dallas, "Lena Horne does it." End of argument.

There's another Lena story, this one involving her second stint at the Cave. Juliette was singing there at the time. She knocked on Lena's dressing room door, introduced herself, and asked if she might have an autograph.

"Certainly," Lena said graciously. "How would you like it signed?"

Then she turned to her maid and said, "Would you sign a picture for Juliette, please?"

It was a different entertainment scene in those days, of course. No fans being hoisted in the air and passed from person to person, no—what do they call them? mosh pits? in the dance halls. As for the clubs like the Cave, dinner was

*The ever-glamorous Lena Horne, guesting on CBC radio. Lena was also a guest at our house, where our fascinated daughter, Dallas, learned to pop her gum "just like Lena."* City of Vancouver Archives CVA A1184 (D2902), Jack Lindsay photo

served but seldom memorable. Nobody cared. They were there for the entertainment. But by the second show at midnight a lot of customers were much the worse for wear, chattering and table-hopping. Things could get out of hand. Those on stage had to live with it or deal with it. Sometimes the reaction could be as entertaining as the show.

Drummer Buddy Rich was known as a man with a terrible temper. Later in his career he became a late-night talk show favourite for the way he chewed on the hosts and sneered at musicians and singers of the day. In his heyday, his showdown with a well-known hooker in Vancouver became an instant legend.

One of the better-known ladies of the evening was a regular at the clubs and liked to, uh, *collect* celebrities, and she didn't take it well when she was rebuffed. One of her targets was Sammy Davis Jr., who was having none of it no matter how hard she tried. So, on his final night at the Cave, she sat at her usual reserved table in front of the stage and read a newspaper through his entire act. But she met her match in Buddy.

When Buddy brought his band to Isy's, she arrived with a party of a half-dozen or so, parked at a table right under his drum set, and never stopped talking. Never mind that other people wanted to hear the band, she just rattled on. Finally, Buddy cracked.

He stopped the band in mid-number, climbed off his stool, walked to the edge of the stage above her and shouted:

"I don't come to your place of business and interrupt whatever the hell it is that *you* do. Now, quit interrupting mine or get the %$*&! outa here!"

Buddy never changed. In Mel Tormé's memoir, *It Wasn't All Velvet*, he discusses his final conversation with Rich, in hospital where Buddy lay dying of a malignant brain tumour. Mel had promised to write Buddy's biography.

"B," I asked, as gently as possible, "How do I write this—warts and all?"

He smiled his first and only smile that day and said "Absolutely. Warts and all…"

Buddy wasn't through yet. As he was being wheeled into the operating room for surgery the next day a nurse asked him if he had any allergies.

"Yeah," Buddy said. "Country and western music."

*He never liked the nickname, but he heard and read it everywhere he performed, including on regular visits to Vancouver. Mel Tormé was The Velvet Fog.*
Glen Erikson photo

Not all acts that played the Cave in the '40s were a success. Take, for instance, Dooley Wilson, famous for playing and singing *As Time Goes By* in *Casablanca* for Ingrid Bergman and Humphrey Bogart.

The scenes with Dooley at the piano were a fake. Dooley wasn't a piano player at all, he was a drummer. I guess they liked his face or his voice or the fact that he was black. Whatever. He was paid $750 to fake the piano playing while Elliott Carpenter sat behind a curtain at another piano and actually made the music. But when the movie turned out to be a blockbuster, somebody got the great idea that Dooley should go on tour. They'd put a piano on the stage, Dooley would walk out, sing a few numbers while he pretended to play the piano while someone else actually played another piano under cover, then walk off stage. I don't know how it worked in other cities, but at the Cave, not so good. You see, the Cave had a balcony. People up there had a clear view of Dooley's hands. They could see he wasn't playing a note. Kind of took the edge off his act.

Oh, if the walls and fake stalactites hanging from the Cave's grotto-style ceiling could have spoken and confessed everything before the demolition in 1981, what stories they could have told. Some would be unbelievable, but true, like the story of the one-hit wonder singer and pianist who had to hide out between shows because he'd upset the Mafia and a local hit man had been assigned to put a bullet in him or make him a permanent part of a freeway project.

They could tell us of laughter and tears, smashes and flops, and the days when four-letter words were shocking and black entertainers would knock 'em dead on stage but weren't good enough to stay in the hotels not more than a block away.

In these anything-goes days, when television eats up material and brings the liberalized, shock-proof world to the living room, it's easy to forget how different things once were, and not that long ago. No one gives any thought to the race or colour of entertainers. But when Sammy Davis Jr. appeared at the Cave in the '50s, he slept on a couch in the Green Room of the Penthouse because downtown hotels weren't yet ready to accommodate blacks, the excuse being that their presence might offend visiting Americans.

*It was supposed to be a shot of Ginger Rogers and me at the International Plaza Hotel, but one of Ginger's fans couldn't resist jumping into the picture, earning a semi-hug he probably never forgot.* Simon Terlinden photo

There were exceptions. Louis Armstrong is said to have checked into the Hotel Vancouver. (A year or so later, when he returned for another show, he stayed at the Hotel Devonshire, where a newspaper photographer got a shot of him sitting on his luggage in the lobby that was so good it was used as the cover art for one of his record albums.) Still, when the Hotel Georgia agreed, after much urging by local entertainment impresario Hugh Pickett, to take a chance and accommodate Nat King Cole a few years later it was done with much trepidation. Cole was so *black*. People in the lobby would *notice*.

Pickett, who routinely found accommodation for black entertainers in hotels out of the downtown core and often put them up in his own home when he couldn't, was adamant. "Take a chance," he urged Georgia manager Bill Hudson. He did, and the sky did not fall.

Today, you'd be hard pressed to find stand-up comics on the cable channels who don't use the ultimate four-letter word (no, I do not mean "love") as noun, verb, adjective and adverb. Ask them to spell "mother" and they'd probably end it with a hyphen. But in 1962, when comic Lenny Bruce brought his then ground-breaking off-colour act to Isy's, the morality squad shut him down after two nights, citing a city bylaw which "did prohibit or prevent any lewd or immoral performance or exhibition."

Isy was told his operating licence would be suspended if Bruce performed again, and he cancelled the rest of the engagement. When the Inquisition Coffee House offered to showcase Bruce for the balance of his contracted stay, management got the same warning: do it, and we shut you down. Bruce flew home, a trail of adjectives involving Vancouver in his wake.

The ghosts that surely haunt the spots where the Cave, the Palomar and so many other entertainment landmarks once stood could fill the hours with tales of the way things were and the way they changed.

In the '40s, a lot of people lived poor and scrambled. You could make money if you caught on with a band—

*In* Laugh-In's *heyday nobody drew bigger laughs than comedian Arte Johnson, who was just as funny off stage as on.* Stephen Miller photo

average salary for a three-hour gig, 9 p.m. to midnight: $6 per man. A steady job six nights a week in one of the ballrooms could earn you $45–$50, the band leader getting 50 percent more. At a time when a room could be had for $10 a week, $35 a week was good money. Theatre musicians, the kings of our profession, could up that to $50 or $55. But there were always more musicians than jobs. You had to be flexible—which brings us to a man whose name has been lost through the ages when it should stand as a memorial to those days when hotel gigs were the best of all, hotel managers were kings, band leaders mere serfs hustling for employment and a manager might pick the hotel's entertainment based not on trends of the day but on music that he himself loved.

The way the story goes, Stan Patton and his band were auditioning in Toronto for a Canadian Pacific official in charge of selecting orchestras for the chain's hotels, trying to land a summer job playing at the Banff Springs Hotel. Others who knew the scene there had warned Stan in advance that the band had better know *The Blue Danube Waltz* and *Home on the Range* because they were the man's favourites, he was bound to ask to hear them, and if the band couldn't produce them to his satisfaction all hope for the gig would be gone.

Sure enough, about fifteen minutes into the audition the exec conceded that the band sounded pretty good "with none of that *cremendos* stuff." (Best guess was that he meant *"crescendos."*) Then he asked Stan to play *The Blue Danby* and followed that with a request for *Home on the Ranch*.

*Newly restored to all its former glory, the Commodore Ballroom reopened in 2000. One of its short-lived but sell-out attractions: Sunday afternoon tea dances featuring the Dal Richards Orchestra.* Dave Roels photo

That's one aspect of the business that's never changed and isn't likely to: you are always at the whim and mercy of the people running the place where you're playing, which is fair enough since it's their dough. But when you sell out and it's *still* not good enough...

Flash forward a second to 2000: The Commodore Ballroom had just undergone a complete facelift and restoration to return it to its old-time glory and make it once again the finest live music venue in the city. Just before it reopened, I got a call. The ballroom had a rock band policy at the time and had booked a couple for the Friday–Saturday–Sunday opening weekend. But management was getting calls from old-time Commodore fans (the Shaughnessy and UBC crowd, we called them) who wanted to revisit their memories and see what had been done to their favourite dance hall. Did I have any ideas?

When they told me Sunday afternoon was available I suggested a tea dance. "What's a tea dance?" they asked. I explained that, in addition to bar service, they would serve tea in cups and saucers, finger sandwiches, cake, etc. They agreed, and did some advertising.

I'll never forget the sight when I went to work that Sunday morning. The Commodore hadn't opened and the dance was to run from noon to 4 p.m., but the lineup extended down the block and around the corner. Management was amazed that they had a full house. Tea dances, they saw, were the way to go. We had four or five more, all really successful. Now it was time for something special. Mart Kenney, leader of the country's No. 1 band, the Glenn Miller of Canada's '30s and '40s, would celebrate his ninetieth birthday March 7. What better reason to hold a tea dance? The ads went out, the buzz started, a full house was assured—and three or four days before the dance, management changed its mind.

"But, *why?*" I asked. "We'd fill the place again." The answer was a testimonial to the madcap side of the business.

"Sure, a full house," they said. "But we have to rent tea cups and saucers and bring in a caterer for the sandwiches and cakes and stuff, and the tea dance crowd doesn't buy beer, which is how we make our money. You want us to hold it, find $3,000."

*Happy ninetieth birthday, Mart Kenney. The Canadian band leader whose Western Gentlemen were a musical byword for generations, is congratulated by another legend, Vancouver broadcaster Jack Webster.*

I went to Ray Smith, by then the retired CEO and president at MacBlo and explained the problem, asking not for money but for ideas.

"Let me speak to Jimmy [Pattison]," he said. They came up with the $3,000. The tea dance sold out, was a big success, but didn't quite break even. I absorbed the shortfall in the orchestra payment. Happy birthday, Mart. Farewell, tea dances at the Commodore.

I mentioned that in the '40s most everyone lived poor and scrambled. By the '70s all that had changed. Now everybody lived rich but hardly anyone was making any money. Even the movers and shakers were forever betting on the come. I remember Isy asking me to stay a few minutes after the show. He had to talk to me. "I've got a great act I can book for two weeks," he said. "Can you lend me $10,000?" At that time I probably could have, but I figured it would be safer to go down to the Inner Harbour and throw the dough in the ocean, or to set fire to it. I declined with thanks. Not that I thought Isy was dishonest, but show biz sometimes was.

It was a time for schemers, dreamers and entrepreneurs— which by now I'd learned was a French word meaning "I've got an idea if you've got the money." Some made it, most didn't, but everybody tried—which, come to think of it, is a pretty good definition of the life we all loved and chose to live. Still is.

# Put Your Hands Together For...

*"I got the horse right here..."*

Roy McLeod, Beacon Theatre Manager, 1946.

There is a legend about Frank Baker that goes something like this:

He was caught in a traffic jam on Vancouver's Lions Gate Bridge. Some poor, distressed soul had climbed over the railing and was threatening to jump while police tried in vain to coax him to climb down.

Frank sat for a while, drumming his fingers on the wheel. Finally, he got out, opened the trunk of his car, pulled out his trumpet—and blew *Taps*.

It is a tale, sadly unsubstantiated, that over the years has taken on a life of its own. The one reason I think it could be true is that I sat in the stands in Toronto's Varsity Stadium in 1964 watching the BC Lions play Hamilton Tiger-Cats for the Canadian Football League championship and the Grey Cup, which Hamilton had won the year before by beating the Lions in Vancouver. Frank was holding his trumpet. Every time a TiCat lay injured on the field or was slow getting to his feet, Frank would stand up and blow *I'll Be Glad When You're Dead, You Rascal, You.*

Frank was one of an inexhaustible supply of characters in and around the city's entertainment business, a man who, for all that he accomplished, basically was famous for being famous. He and partner Frank Bernard bought the Georgian Towers hotel and in it opened two restaurants, the Colonial House and the Top of the Towers, where, resplendent in his trademark white suit, he blew *Taps* at sundown on the trumpet he'd learned to play at the Four Square Gospel Church. It was one of the things that made people think of him as a character, and he played on it shamelessly. His West Vancouver restaurant, The Attic, was famous for its Tiffany lamps, Lance Harrison's dance band, and the Aston Martin automobile parked out front, the one used as a promotional vehicle for the US release of the James Bond movie, *Thunderball.*

Let me tell you about a few of the others.

Husk O'Hare and his Genial Gentlemen of the Air were one of the dance bands appearing every night at the LaSalle Hotel in Chicago and carried live on radio station WGN, which we could pick up out here late at night. At least once during the show he'd say something like "If you want to hear *your* song played *on the air,* send a copy to Husk at the hotel along with $5…" I don't know how many $5 bills he got, but I don't recall hearing many original songs on his show.

— ❖ —

In these days of strobe lighting and light banks everywhere it may be hard to believe, but the Cave initially operated with one spotlight. It was run by a guy we called "Two-for Joe," because he was forever peddling tickets to the poorer draws, two for the price of one.

Once in a while, Two-for's girlfriend would show up and sit at one of the tables waiting for him. Often she was with some guy. Two-for would check the table from time to time, and if he thought anything untoward was happening he would swing the spotlight onto her table, click it off and on a couple of times, then swing it back to the stage, where the performer stood there wondering what the hell had just happened. Don't know why he wasn't fired. Maybe management had a soft spot for true love.

And then there was the Professor—William John Francis, it was said, although no one knew for sure. The Professor was a pianist, a gaunt, unshaven raconteur in rags, a scrounger who lived in rooms somewhere in the west end of town and seemed to have no visible means of support. Some said he was a remittance man—a socially unacceptable guy shipped west by a wealthy family and supported on the condition that he not return.

Who knows? In the city he was just a character—and the finest gate-crasher around. Let a celebrity hit town, including royalty, and the Professor would be there to shake a hand or yell, "Hello, Your Highness." There wasn't a stage show he missed, a dressing room he couldn't crash. And he loved the Kitsilano Boys Band.

We'd do a concert and he'd be at the stage door, his ever-present stack of newspapers under his arm. "Great show tonight, boys," he'd say. "I gave you eighty-eight points."

In his own way, the Professor was loved. When he died of a heart attack—at the piano in a club, having just finished his rendition of Paul Anka's *Diana*—his pallbearers included radio man Vic Waters, who'd made him a frequent guest on his nighttime radio show, and Jack Wasserman, who knew all the offbeats in town and considered the Professor one of the best.

By the time he got to the Commodore in the '50s as part of a show called Stars of the '20s with Sophie Tucker and Fifi Dorsey, Rudy Vallée already qualified as ancient history. So when he came back to the ballroom in 1972 for a one-night stand, no one knew quite what to expect, and no one expected what we got.

Here was a man generally credited with pioneering the crooner style of singing; a man who sang into a hand-held megaphone in the early days of his career because the electric microphone hadn't yet been invented; a man generally credited with saving the sheet music industry in the hungry '30s because his songs were some of the few selling; the host of radio's first variety show, the *Fleischman Hour* in 1928, where he was the first to hire black musicians like Louis Armstrong and Ethel Waters as guest performers.

My band had been hired to back him up. Rudy obviously was faking it, counting on his memories rather than his voice. He and the Commodore crowd clearly weren't a good mix. They didn't know his music or many of the people in his stories, who were all two generations back.

Then he said: "I'd like to conduct Morton Gould's arrangement of *Ebb Tide*." This was news to us. There'd been no mention of *Ebb Tide* during rehearsal. So we're scrambling through the book looking for the arrangement when Rudy pushes a button on a tape recorder and suddenly the sound of Morton Gould's *Ebb Tide* is flooding the ballroom.

Then he pulls a baton from his pocket and begins conducting the music as though he was Morton himself. And that was the climax of his show, the big finish, serious as hell: Rudy Vallée, the legend of the '20s, waving a baton in front of a tape recorder.

I enjoyed Rudy's company. During his stay he had a suite at the Hotel Georgia where I was director of sales. I spent quite a bit of time with him and his recently acquired wife, listening to his stories of starting up in the '20s and '30s, including his deal with a brewery that sponsored his radio show for a while in which he was to receive a case of liquor every week during the run of his show. Rudy didn't drink much himself, but he was close with a dime and I guess the liquor cut expenses when he entertained at his Hollywood home. As the cases mounted, he had the tennis court dug up and converted to storage space for the booze.

We backed up a lot of visiting entertainers over the years, few more intriguing than the legendary Bob Hope, a gentleman, a philanthropist whose Desert Classic golf tournament raised millions for charitable causes, a performer so determined to give his best that he sent his writers a couple of days early into any city in which he was booked in order to work the area's topics of the day into his stand-up routine.

A consummate professional, Bob Hope. But when it came to money he was, well, *close.* In the heyday of network radio, Jack Benny had a carefully constructed shtick that portrayed him as a man who squeezed every penny so tightly that the portrait of Abraham Lincoln on the face got a headache. In real life, Bob Hope might have wrestled him for the coin.

His musical director arrived a day early for Hope's Vancouver appearance and ran us through an exhaustive program, of which we wound up using about half. He brought with him Hope's musical library, a book that clearly had seen better days.

We opened it and began the rehearsal. But first:

"Cut from B to D," the director said. "Bob doesn't dance any more."

Then:

"From letter G to J is out, because Bob doesn't sing that high any more."

The book was full of chicken scratches where musicians in the past had scratched out some bits and added others. Judging by their number, the book had been used for years. Making new copies would have been simple and not all that costly, but Hope preferred to stick with the old one.

Hope was in his early 80s by then. Sitting at the head table he looked small and subdued, but when he stood up to speak and the spotlight was on him, I swear he *grew*. Just like that, he was Bob Hope, the comic legend, doing what he was born to do and loving every second of it.

I noticed it again after the show. Hope was sitting alone at a table, withdrawn and quiet. To me he seemed *lonesome*. But when I went over to say hello he brightened right up. Just like that, the old vaudevillian, radio and movie star was back. I wasn't talking to an old man, I was talking to a legend.

For another Vancouver engagement, Hope's deal called for a $50,000 fee in advance plus fuel costs for the trip up in his private jet. When he arrived at the hotel he turned to Peter Legge of Canada Wide Media and asked for his cheque for the fuel. Peter had assumed he'd get an invoice later. "No," Hope said pleasantly, "I'd like it now." In the end, Heather Parker, Canada Wide VP Operations, wrote him a personal cheque for $5,200.

The show, incidentally, was a smash.

Jack Benny, by the way, had a deeply rooted affection for Vancouver in general and the Orpheum in particular. He'd played the theatre in the '20s, appearing on the same bill as the Marx Brothers, and it was here he met his future wife and comedic partner, Mary Livingston (née Sadie Marks), born in Seattle but raised in Vancouver. At the request of Hugh Pickett of the Save the Orpheum committee, when the venerable showplace seemed doomed to conversion to a movie house Jack campaigned front and centre. Benny brought his radio show to town in 1944—Mary,

119

Phil Harris, Rochester, Dennis Day, announcer Don Wilson and special guest, actor Ray Milland. I assembled the local musicians for the show, conducted by Benny's musical director, Mahlon Merrick. So I was there when Jack went into his Orpheum routine:

Jack: You know, Mary, being in Vancouver brings back memories for me, too. When I was in Vaudeville, I played the Orpheum Theatre many times. Did you know that?

Mary: Did I *know* that? Jack, every time you played here, did you notice a little girl in the third row in the aisle seat with long blonde pigtails and a pink ribbon in her hair?

Jack: Well, I'll be darned! Was that you?

Mary: No, that was my mother.

Jack: Now cut that out!

Rehearsals are supposed to get everyone on the same page and smooth out the bumps. Usually, they do. But not always. Las Vegas comedian Shecky Greene was in town for a celebrity roast fundraising dinner. Rehearsal started pretty well. Shecky did his opening monologue, told a joke or two, but somehow lost his place or his train of thought, got mad at us, threw his microphone and stalked off, never to return. He left a note at his hotel. It read: "I owe you one."

Joe Miller was a tailor who hung around the Arctic, the Penthouse and other local clubs and had a business card that read:

## JOE MILLER
Solid Sender of
Sartorial Splendour

Joe had some pretty good connections on the club scene and wound up making clothes for some of the visiting stars. One night he invited Vern Thomson, the hat check chick at the Arctic, to have dinner with him at a beautiful restaurant on Georgia called Royce's Cloud Room. She was stunned to discover that Joe's other guests at the table were the pop vocal group the Four Aces, who had several big hits like *Garden in the Rain, Tell Me Why* and *Three Coins in the Fountain*. But, for all his claims to be a solid sender, Joe would most prefer to be known as the winner of the Friday night jitterbug contests Ivan Ackery threw at the Orpheum, even though Joe was the oldest guy on the stage. But he never lost an opportunity to sell a suit.

Lorraine and I took a friend from Montreal to the Penthouse one night after the show at the Roof. We met Joe there, and our friend admired his suit. "No problem," Joe said. "I can make you one just like it." And off we went in the dead of night to his shop, where he took the measurements and assured us that the suit would be ready very soon, delivered to Montreal.

Our friend phoned from Montreal in a couple of weeks. No suit. I went looking for Joe on Granville Street. "Just being cut," he assured me. Sure enough, the suit did get there eventually. Joe was an honest man. Perhaps, though, just a bit too enthusiastic a salesman.

— ❖ —

But that was the way it was: people hustled and scuffled as best they could and made do with what that hustle and scuffle provided.

Take Roy McLeod, manager of the Beacon Theatre on East Hastings Street. The Beacon featured vaudeville acts— sopranos, comics, acrobats, dog acts, guys doing rope tricks, whatever. One of the performers on the circuit in 1946 was Roy Rogers, and now movies' King of the Cowboys was coming to McLeod's theatre—with his wonder horse, Trigger. Clearly, this called for some publicity, preferably free. McLeod thought a while, then asked himself a question: Where was the most unlikely place in Vancouver where he could get a publicity shot of Roy and Trigger?

"The Panorama Roof!" he thought.

He approached Hotel Vancouver management and talked them into smuggling Trigger and Roy up the freight elevator to the Roof and letting them walk out into the middle of the dance floor. The horse would be no problem. Trigger was on stage all the time these days. Management agreed, Roy and Trigger posed for pictures in front of my band with a couple of customers from ringside. The picture made all the papers, even hit the wire service.

Roy McLeod smiled. His Beacon show had its publicity— and it hadn't cost him a cent.

In the mid-'50s I was personally involved with another cowboy hero, the Cisco Kid himself. The Gyros, with whom I've been associated for 60-some years, needed an attraction for their campaign to raise funds to construct playgrounds

Roy Rogers and Trigger had many adventures, but none stranger than the one in 1946, when the King of the Cowboys and his golden palomino made a guest appearance on the dance floor at the Panorama Roof to publicize a vaudeville appearance at the Beacon Theatre.

in the area, and who better than the star of the popular kids' TV show, the Cisco Kid?

I was in charge of squiring Cisco—aka Duncan Renaldo—around town. He appeared at Safeway stores signing autographs for kids and, riding his famous horse, Diablo, at the PNE's horse show building, where he fired his pistol in the air as he rode into the arena.

What with his interest in horses, I thought he'd like to drop in to the Hastings Park race course, so I took him up to the announcer's booth where he would get a great view of Vancouver and could watch the veteran Jack Short call the races. I don't know how impressed he was with the city, but he certainly was impressed with the way Jack made the race calls.

Ah, Cisco!

Art Cameron was resident manager of the Hotel Vancouver for decades, a genial sort whose personality and attentiveness were major factors in landing convention attendees and visiting sports teams. He was a man of such dry wit and quick recognition and response to a funny line or situation that he could have been a professional gag writer for radio or TV. Indeed, he did provide material for the likes of his personal friends Bob Hope, Jack Benny, Phil Harris, Edgar Bergen and other entertainers who would call in advance of their Vancouver gigs to ask him to provide a few topical lines on the local scene. He was a regular contributor to a weekly CBC show called *Stag Party*, produced in Studio One (at that time in the hotel) and starring Vancouver comic Alan Young, who would go on to great fame and a permanent spot in Trivia contests. ("Who played Wilbur in the TV show, *Mr. Ed*?")

Art had a room in the hotel and frequently invited Lorraine and me down for drinks and conversation after the Roof closed. We were sitting there one night, the window blinds up, when we looked across at the corresponding room on the other wing of the hotel's H-shaped layout and saw a man and a women enthusiastically enjoying each other's

*He would soon go on to worldwide TV sitcom fame as Wilbur, the semi-hapless owner of the talking horse, Mr. Ed, but Canadian Alan Young got his start as a stand-up comic and radio performer in Vancouver.*

company. Art had no trouble figuring out the room number in the other wing. He picked up the phone and called over.

When the couple disengaged so the guy could answer the phone, Art put on his best Charlton Heston voice and thundered:

"This is God speaking! You've got thirty seconds to get that woman out of that room!"

We watched the poor guy leap off the bed and gaze wildly around the room, not knowing what to think. But he *did* look up.

Or, consider the hat check chick.

Vern Thomson was working across the street from the Arctic Club in a hair and scalp shop, where bald men took hair restoration treatments in the vain hope that the old roots would resurrect. The success rate was not what you'd call high. The Arctic was a second-floor spot over Leonard's Café on Pender between Granville and Howe. When her shift ended at 7 p.m., Vern and another girl from the scalp shop would drop over to the club to listen to the Chris Gage Trio. Then one night the scalp shop owner came into town and shut the place down.

They were sitting in the club mulling their unemployment when owner Bob Mitten asked if she'd like to fill in for a few days as a hat check chick. The regular chick, a girl named Roma Hearn, had a chance to sing at Theatre Under the Stars (TUTS) and he needed a replacement. "Just for a few days," he cautioned.

Roma, of course, used the TUTS break as a launching pad for an illustrious career on stage and in radio and TV, which left the Arctic Club job open full time.

Just like that, the young scalp masseuse, eighteen years old and three years short of legal drinking age, was a full-time hat check chick in one of the city's busiest clubs with emerging stars like Pat Suzuki and Rolf Harris appearing regularly.

For a young and single girl it was educational. On weekdays the luncheon crowd was mainly boisterous businessmen with their girlfriends or Howe Street rounders, blowhards who wore or drove everything they owned. The laughter was loud, the tips great. On weekends the same guys would bring their wives out for the evening, the tips petered out and it was as though the hat check chick was invisible.

Vern moved on, got a secretarial job with an insurance company, married, moved to Winnipeg, came back when the marriage didn't work out, and got a job with ICBC setting up credit collections. Then a friend asked her to look at the books of the Candy Store disco on Burrard Street, which was about sixty grand in the glue. She bought it in 1976, cleaned it up, ran off the rowdies and filled the place every night.

When she decided to redesign and move her club across the street to the Royal Centre mall below the Hyatt Regency hotel, she drew up her plan on a cocktail napkin in the bar at the Hyatt and was incensed when the city planners demanded something a little more detailed. She went to a well-known home designer, presented her napkin, and asked for a set of plans. The club—restaurant by day, disco by night—was another roaring success for about three years until the disco craze began to flame out. She tried roller disco, western disco, fashion shows, anything she thought might have a chance, then sold and retired. The place was gone in six months.

But, see what I mean? The entertainment scene was vibrant and full of people who weren't afraid to take a chance. No doubt they're still out there. But, somehow, I doubt they're having as much fun.

# Nights of Elegance

*"Dal can read a room. He can stand out there and know right away what kind of crowd he's playing to and how to get them going, when to relax and when to step on the gas. I can see the dance floor fill up and just stay full because people are having such a good time nobody wants to sit down. I don't think his book or his arrangements are any better than any other band might have. It's his presence, his command. He makes it so comfortable to play for him, and when things are going well he gets this ear-to-ear grin plastered all over his face. All those years, and still nobody's having more fun than he is."*

Gary Mussatto, drums.

Against all odds and logic, given its history, the new Hotel Vancouver opened on May 27, 1939, just in time for the royal tour of the new king, George VI, and his consort, Elizabeth. That, in turn, led to the opening of the supper room, as dinner dancing facilities were called, that became the epitome of elegance for Vancouver's society set and my working home for twenty-five years, the Panorama Roof.

It began as a Canadian National Railway hotel to compete with the rival Canadian Pacific Railway's Hotel Vancouver on Georgia and Granville streets on the property currently occupied by the Eaton Centre. (Now *there* was a beautiful hotel. It housed the Crystal Ballroom and the Spanish Grill nightclub. The lobby was called Peacock Alley, as in New York's Waldorf Astoria. But it closed after only thirty years of operation.) Construction on the new hotel began in 1928, ran headlong into the Depression and was halted for ten years, the building shell sitting unfinished. Meanwhile, the Depression had also hit the old Hotel Vancouver, which was sitting with too many empty rooms. The plan to solve both companies' problems was ambitious but ludicrous: the two railroads joined forces to finance and finish the new hotel, and devised a system in which they would alternate as overseers of the operation on an annual basis.

It was farcical. Jim Coleman, the nationally syndicated Toronto sports columnist whose father was president of the CPR, would stay in the best suite in the place in the CPR years and find another hotel when the CNR managed. But that was how the railroads were run: the railway or no way and nobody get *in* the way. There was even a Depression-era joke about it:

The manager of the Hotel Frontenac in Quebec City calls in his second-in-command. "We have to cut staff," he says. "It's just fundamentally unsound to have this many employees. Where do we start firing?"

In 1939, Vancouver got a new luxury tourist venue, the Hotel Vancouver and a "supper room," as they were called then, that became the place to be for generations and my long-time working home, the Panorama Roof.
City of Vancouver Archives Hot P70

They decide on the silver polisher, his job not being essential. "Bring him in," the manager says.

The silver polisher is brought before the manager and given the news. He does not seem upset. "Oh, *thank you*, sir, *"Thank you!"* he says.

"You don't understand," the manager says. "How can you be so happy? I just *fired* you."

"I know, sir," says the silver polisher. "I thought you were going to *kill* me!"

None of this mattered a hoot to the Vancouver public, many of whom had fond memories of the old hotel's grandeur and wondered how this new, oft-delayed successor could ever come close to matching the splendour that had been the Crystal Ballroom. But the wait was justified. The new $12-million edifice was gorgeous and the Panorama Roof sheer elegance.

Picture yourself and your date coming to the hotel for a night of dining and dancing on the Roof in the opening weeks.

You walk through a gorgeously appointed lobby to the elevators where uniformed elevator girls lift you to the

*Vocalist and pianist Beryl Boden succeeded Juliette in 1943 and became the first Mrs. Dal Richards in 1945. We had good times, but the big time in New York beckoned, and Beryl left for the Big Apple to pursue a big-time singing career.*

fifteenth floor. You step out into luxury. The lobby is mirrored floor to ceiling at one end with a view window on the other overlooking Point Grey and Kitsilano. It's evening, so the city lights below are sparkling.

You go up three steps to be greeted by the *maître d'* in white tie and tails and the head waiter in tuxedo. You pause while your name is located on the reservation list. At this point you are three steps above the dance floor, which begins a few feet ahead. You look across it to the band at the other end. Behind the band is a splendid backdrop, a rear wall covered with alternating mahogany panels and luxurious drapery. You gaze to the right where windows twenty feet high offer a panoramic view south over Kitsilano and the University of BC. You gaze left and see the North Shore mountains. The effect is mesmerizing, so much so that you're only dimly aware of being guided to your table, either on that level or down three steps to the area around the dance floor itself.

You're seated, and you and your date gaze around the room, which seats 200. The walls are covered in striking tapestry—red, black and white in design. The pillars are covered with tiny mirrors, one inch by a half inch. Back of the bandstand, although probably you don't notice, given the opulence of your surroundings, is a light console controlling every light in the room—one band member assigned to operate it so that the lighting is appropriate for the music being played. So, you have the view and the changing colours playing over the dancers. You pick up the menu and consider your options. On the left-hand side is the *table d'hôte*, featuring a starter (usually a fruit cocktail), main course (cold meat plate or something light and hot), dessert and coffee. Price (wait for it): $1. On the menu's right-hand side, should you really want to live rich and dine *à la carte*, you can order steak for $2.

So there you are, you and your date, in the most elegant room in the city, dancing to the Len Hopkins orchestra from the Chateau Laurier hotel in Ottawa, who opened the Roof, or the Mart Kenney orchestra that succeeded him, or sitting back listening to their featured vocalist. There was no admission or cover charge. Your meal has cost a buck apiece, or maybe two. If you brought in a flask, you've bought ice and mixer. But that's it. Your evening is going to cost you $10 tops, and you're mingling with the *crème de la crème* of Vancouver society—the Shaughnessy Set, as we called them. On prestige alone you've already scored big points with your date, and the evening is young. Is this living, or what?

By the time my band began its stint at the Roof in 1940, *table d'hôte* prices had rocketed up to $2, then to $2.50. Rummaging around recently in some memorabilia boxes, I found a 1953 Panorama Roof menu. The cover charge is listed at $3.50, with a bracketed reminder that "$1.75 of this charge is exempt from the BC Social Security and Municipal Aid Tax." When we played the New Year's Eve gig in 1954 the tickets sold for $7.50 apiece. A 1959 Holiday Festivities card lists Christmas and New Year's Eve dinners at $4.50 and reminds one and all that "the Dal Richard's [sic] orchestra will be featured."

From opening night on, it was the talk of the town, the place to be and be seen. Vancouver's daily newspapers, the *Sun, Province* and *News-Herald*, would send society reporters—

Marie Moreau, Pat Proud, Pat Wallace, Al Williamson—on Saturday nights to compile lists of the big names in attendance, lists that ran in the next edition. Jack Scott, the celebrated *Vancouver Sun* columnist, wrote one on our rehearsal. No one had seen anything like it. To say it was unequalled in Canada was to shortchange it. The truth was, the Roof would stand up against any such room anywhere. When Lorraine and I travelled, the first thing we'd do was hit the big rooms. The only ones you could put on a par were the Coconut Grove in the Ambassador Hotel in Los Angeles or the Starlight Roof of the Waldorf Astoria in New York.

In those years it was open only two nights a week—Wednesday's from 7:30 to 10:30, when the dress code was relaxed because people were coming directly from their places of business; and Saturday from 9 p.m. to midnight,

*Lorraine and I loved to travel and hit the clubs everywhere we went. That's how we met band leader Freddy Martin, at the Coconut Grove in the Ambassador Hotel in Los Angeles.*

which, for about a year, was strictly black tie and formal dresses. That didn't last long. It was wartime, and more and more men and women in uniform were in attendance. Somehow it didn't seem right, captains of industry and the city's movers and shakers showing up to party in black tie when young people in uniform were there, some for farewell parties with loved ones and friends before heading to war zones from which so many would not return.

There was always a waiting list, and a Wednesday night list of regulars who only phoned if they *weren't* coming. Friends would phone me. "Dal, can you get me in?" Table hopping was ongoing because everyone knew everyone else. The Roof was the in crowd's destination for birthday parties, anniversaries and coming-of-age celebrations. When teenagers were taken to the Roof, they knew it was a pronouncement that they were now considered adults. A young girl taken to the Roof for dinner and dancing knew that her beau was serious. Many a marriage proposal was made to our music. If you asked a girl out for a night at the Roof, she knew you were serious. Families brought children who learned to dance by standing on their parent's toes.

For visiting celebrities, a Roof drop-in was *de rigueur*, some to party, some to be noticed. Rudy Vallée and Eddie Cantor would pause at the entranceway until I saw them from the bandstand and recognized their presence.

*"Hi, Rudy! Good to see you! Rudy Vallée's here, ladies and gentlemen!"*

*"Eddie Cantor! Hi, Eddie! Come on in!"*

Bing Crosby, on the other hand, would try to slide in with his party unobtrusively, and soon someone would come to me and say, "Please don't mention that Bing is here." I didn't have to, of course. Everyone in the place knew Bing was there.

Business was so good that a Friday night opening was added in 1943. To help promote it, I concocted a scheme in which UBC sororities, in exchange for a $5 donation for their Red Cross fund, were asked to choose one of their members who could sing to come do a song with my band. Naturally, their friends and fellow sorority members had to come to heckle or to cheer them on. Eventually, the Roof became a Tuesday-through Saturday operation. As a band, we changed with the times. During the war years we featured the brass section and concentrated on swing. In the '50s I added strings to produce a softer, dinner-oriented sound. It seemed like the party was never going to end.

That didn't mean I stopped hustling for business. During Lorraine's years at the Roof we developed our own version of *Upstairs, Downstairs*.

Friday and Saturday were the most popular nights of the week for functions in the Pacific Ballroom down on the first floor. I had an arrangement with food and beverage manager John Helders to inform me of upcoming bookings along with the name of the person who'd made the reservation. I would phone that person and ask whether they'd made arrangements for music for their function. At that early date the answer was usually no. "Well," I'd ask, "how would you like to have the Dal Richards orchestra?"

"You're playing at The Roof," they'd reply.

"I have an orchestra under the direction of Al Reusch who plays my arrangements," I'd explain. "A couple of times during the evening, Lorraine comes down to the ballroom for twenty minutes. I do the same thing at other times. We sing some songs, the music's the same. It's the Dal Richards orchestra. You can even print it on your tickets."

We worked that maybe a couple of times a month for about ten years. We were never both away at the same time and we usually managed it so we were on a break at the Roof. The service elevator to the main floor was behind the Roof bandstand, so getting out quickly was no problem. As soon as Al saw one of us coming, he'd pull out the music for either Lorraine's vocals or mine. On the rare occasions when I didn't make it back to the Roof before the break ended, my pianist, Bud Henderson, would conduct until I got back. No harm, no foul. The money was good, and both audiences went away happy. In show biz, nothing's more important than that.

Come next New Year's Eve at the River Rock Casino, I will lead the orchestra in *Auld Lang Syne* for the seventy-fifth consecutive year. It never gets auld. Still, I have to admit that we've come a long way since my old Kits Band buddy, Jack Bensted, arranged our first such gig the year I graduated from Magee.

We had a six-piece group we called the Living Room Band because that's where we practised, in band members' families' living rooms. Jack was dickering with some guy to play a New Year's Eve gig in a meeting room with some space around Main and Broadway for $6 per man. Nothing

*Opposite: In 1964 we put out an LP called* Dance Date with Dal *with my Hotel Vancouver orchestra, featuring Lorraine on vocals.*

Dance Date with Dal

DAL & LORRAINE

was carved in stone. Then Jack got another offer to bring the band to a public rental basement below the Silver Slipper Ballroom—at $10 a man. We accepted, then went to inform the first guy that, sorry, we had a better offer. He did not take it well.

*Party hats, noise-makers, music, crowded dance floors, the countdown to midnight, and* Auld Lang Syne—*New Year's Eve dances have been a huge part of my life. The thrill never dies. At the centre of the photo, sitting on the piano, is singer Lynne McNeil (Hotel Vancouver, early '80s).*

"I'll see you never play another New Year's Eve dance in Vancouver again!" he shouted. It didn't turn out quite that way.

New Year's Eve was always an exciting time, but in the Roof years it could also get awfully tense during our live broadcasts. We were the final segment of the cross-Canada CBC *Dance Parade*, which began with the Don Warner orchestra from the Nova Scotian hotel in Halifax, moved

on to the Queen Elizabeth hotel in Montreal with the Denny Vaughan orchestra, then to the Imperial Room of the Royal York hotel in Toronto with Moxie Whitney's orchestra, from there to Bob Moyer's orchestra in Regina, from there to the McDonald hotel in Edmonton with Mac Cameron's orchestra and, finally, to the Roof for our big finish. The timing was precise: each segment to last exactly 29 minutes and 40 seconds, leaving 20 seconds for the sign-off. (Once I was listening to an old tape of Moxie's Toronto segment and thought I recognized the announcer's voice. It turned out to be Lloyd Robertson, now national anchor and senior editor for CTV news.)

Years later when I was listening to a tape of one of those old broadcasts, to my surprise I heard the announcer sign off with "We now turn you over to Len Chapple, who will describe the celebrations taking place on the streets of Vancouver." Much later, Len married my daughter, Dallas.

The Roof, as it was, is no more, limited now to private functions, the glory days gone. Current manager Mark Andrew made plans for a renovation and grand re-opening in 2010, but the recession put that on the back burner as it did so many other projects. I'm sure if Mark has his way it will happen, and wouldn't it be wonderful to see the queen of the Vancouver supper rooms restored to all her old glory, open to a new generation of dancers and debutantes, a new crop of big-eyed children learning to dance on grandparents' toes as their parents did long ago to the big band music that has never truly faded away? The plans are there and waiting. The ghosts of dances past—and one live old bandleader—surely would applaud.

*Celebrating the reopening of the Panorama Roof in the '70s.*
Kent Kallberg photo

# And the Band Plays On

*"The thing about Dal is, he's not stuck in the past. He presents memories of it, but he's not stuck there. He hires the best and he wants the best out of them, and they respect that."*

Jim Byrnes

The band business is a sort of society within a society with a tinge of craziness all its own, driven by the music it produces but liberally laced with laughter, competitiveness and characters straight out of Damon Runyan.

Let me tell you some stories…

Laughter was seldom in short supply, particularly when there was an out-of-town gig. Put a bunch of entertainers together in cramped quarters in a strange place and oddball things were likely to happen, particularly when the group included the Chris Gage Trio—Chris on piano, Cuddles Johnson on bass and Jimmy Wightman on drums—who thought it was a crime to leave any possible prank unplayed.

In December of 1960 we were part of a troupe flown by army transport to Inuvik to perform at RCAF servicemen's camps. We sat sideways in long rows on both sides of the plane like paratroopers in those war movies, a motley crew to say the least. Lorraine and Eleanor Collins were the vocalists, the Gage trio, my band and vibraphonist Ray Lowdon would provide the music; we had a comedian, the Geneva Calangis dancers and Dr. Grant Gould, uncle of pianist Glen Gould, who was a professional-calibre pianist himself as well as an amateur magician, which I always suspected was his real career preference.

Grant Gould was a naval war hero. During the Normandy Invasion in 1944, his ship was torpedoed while rescuing survivors in the English Channel. Grant was blown off the bridge, but despite severe chest injuries he provided surgical and medical care for crew members, for which he was decorated by King George VI. Back in civilian life, he was my doctor and had treated my ulcer. But he was also Dr. Broadway, a nickname hung on him by the grateful management of the Cave after Judy Garland had complained of a sore throat and was getting ready to bail on the show. Grant was called in, got her back into singing shape, and the show went on. From then on, whenever any Cave performer had any kind of ailment, the cry went out: "Get Dr. Broadway!"

One he couldn't save was Errol Flynn, who died in Gould's apartment on October 14, 1959. He was en route to the airport when he began to experience leg and back pains. His friend, knowing Flynn's friendship with Gould, drove him straight to the doctor's apartment. By then Flynn was feeling better and propped himself against the wall as he regaled guests—there was a party in progress—with tales of Hollywood. He decided to lie down for an hour in Gould's room. He was found on the floor a bit later, already beyond help—the movies' all-time swashbuckler, dead at fifty.

I'd been telling Grant about the upcoming trip to Inuvik. "Hey," he said, "I'd really like to go." I'd considered it, because he'd subbed for Bud Henderson on piano on a couple of occasions on the Roof, and Bud was now unavailable due to a prior commitment. But Chris was a pianist, and taking the trio would provide us a rhythm section of piano, bass and drums. "Well, then," Gordon said, "how about me going along as a magician?" Well, why not? If we needed a doctor, we'd have one right there. He packed his hat and cane—and, who knows, maybe his rabbit?—and away we went.

On the flight up we shared accommodation with a brand new concert piano brought in by the Army especially for our show, which was held at a US Army Air Force base. It wasn't until we prepared to rehearse that someone noticed that the keyboard lid was locked. The key, we learned, was still in the pocket of someone on the plane, which was now on its way back to Vancouver. We had to break the lid to get to the keyboard before we could use the piano.

It was a winter wonderland. In addition to our show for the military personnel we did another at the local high school for residents, many of whom arrived by dog sled. We thought things were going pretty well until we noticed that no one in the audience was paying any attention as Lowdon did his vibes solo. They just kept staring up at the ceiling.

*Dance party in Inuvik, NWT, 1960. We were there to entertain troops stationed at an air base, and the local folks, many of whom arrived by dog sled, who made us feel very welcomed. Our vocalists were Lorraine and Eleanor Collins.*

We finally figured it out. The spotlights were hitting the bars on Ray's vibraphone, which naturally were moving as he hit them. That set the light to bouncing around the ceiling in strange patterns, which the audience apparently found more interesting than the music.

The people were great, though. We had sleigh rides and all kinds of other entertainment. We all slept in one wing of the officer's quarters—the band and the entire show cast, including a saxophone player who slept so deeply a bomb blast wouldn't have shaken him. For Gage and his boys, he was a perfect target. In the middle of the night they lifted his mattress with the guy sound asleep on it, carried it gently out onto the parade ground, lowered it carefully to the ground with its occupant still blissfully asleep—and left it there. He woke up all but frozen to death.

Jimmy Wightman and I often ran into each other in Vancouver and developed a routine almost vaudevillian, based on who could get his hand out first the instant we met. The loser had to put a dime in it. I'm not sure who finished ahead but years later when *Chicago* was in town, Jimmy phoned.

"I'm a little short, Dal," he said. "Can you front me for a couple of tickets?"

How could I say no? Everybody in the business knew at one time or another what it was like to be broke. I got him a couple of tickets for the hottest show in town. He'd have done the same for me. This time, I happened to be the one with the dime.

Benny Goodman was the acknowledged King of Swing. Les Brown's Band of Renown had a huge following, especially after recording *Sentimental Journey* with Doris Day in 1944, when returning servicemen and those waiting to see them again adopted the song and sent it to the top of the *Hit Parade* for sixteen weeks. So is it not logical to think that when these two giants met in Vancouver in the '70s there'd be much back slapping, story swapping and reciprocal good will?

You'd think so, and you'd be dead wrong. I know. I was a guest there and witnessed the collision.

The Four Seasons hotel chain was opening its new Vancouver location and had imported Brown—for a cool $10,000—to play at the opening. Benny Goodman was appearing on the same night at the Queen Elizabeth

Theatre, a show booked by Hugh Pickett. When the show ended, Hugh brought him to the hotel for the festivities. I was standing in the foyer when Hugh made his request.

"Uh, Dal, do you know Les Brown?"

Not well, I admitted, but, yes, I did know him.

"Well, I've got Benny Goodman here with me. Would you see that they meet?"

"I guess so," I said. "But why don't you introduce them?"

"Well, it's like this: Benny and I aren't speaking."

Oops.

Apparently Goodman, who could be a queer duck at times, was upset over something Hugh had said, something about the show, whatever...Now he wasn't talking to Hugh, who was in charge of shepherding him around town. But maybe if he met fellow band great Les Brown...

"Okay," I said.

Hugh brought Goodman over, introduced us, and at intermission I took him over to Brown's table.

"Les," I said jovially, "here's Benny Goodman! Benny, meet Les Brown!"

Les stood up. Goodman ignored him as though he was some kind of band boy, and sat down at the other side of the table. Not one further word was exchanged.

Not that such confrontations are necessarily a bad thing. One collision between trumpeters Miles Davis and Wynton Marsalis actually helped launch the Vancouver International Jazz Festival to the worldwide prominence it now enjoys.

It happened at the Expo Theatre in 1986 on a gorgeous summer night when the fireflies were out, the place was jammed with four thousand jazz fans, and Miles' band was in full swing. Suddenly a figure walks out of the shadows across the stage carrying a trumpet, finds a vacant microphone, and begins to play. It's Marsalis, who's brought his own band into town a few days before its own scheduled show—and he's on the *same stage* with Miles Davis!

Understand, now, in those days there was a bubbling rivalry between the two men generally considered the top trumpeters on the scene: Davis, the veteran, and Marsalis, the young gunslinger. The crowd knows this, as it knows that such a thing couldn't be part of the show. But there they were! *What a bonus!* This was gonna be *great!*

As was often the case, Davis is playing with his back to the audience. He hears the trumpet, realizes something is wrong, raises his hand and brings it down to reduce the band to a whisper so low that people standing sidestage could hear the exchange that followed as Wynton walked over to Davis.

"Miles! It's me, Wynton! Let's play!"

"Get off my stage, mother-%$@&&!"

He turned his back on Marsalis and the crowd, raised his arm, and the band resumed playing as though nothing had happened.

John Orysik, co-founder of the Coastal Jazz and Blues Society, remembers it well for a couple of reasons.

"Wynton was just *crushed*," he recalls. "He walked off the stage head down. Couldn't believe what had just happened. The incident became big news internationally.

It made all the papers, all the jazz shows. And for us, that made all the difference, because now the world knew there was a jazz festival in Vancouver that attracted big names. It gave us a foothold internationally and the Festival has never looked back."

I'm not much for playing the what-might-have-been game, which has always struck me as a waste of time. But here's a tale of one that got away.

It begins in 1930. Bert Lown and his band are getting ready to start the evening at the Biltmore Hotel in New York when two guys from the CBS radio network show up, one carrying a transmitter, the other a microphone and mic stand. "Doing a live remote broadcast in thirty minutes, Bert," the guy with the mic says. "What's your theme song?"

"What's a theme song?" Bert asks, mystified.

"Lombardo has *Auld Lang Syne* in the Grill Room at the Roosevelt Hotel," the guy says. "Wayne King over at the Aragon Ballroom in Chicago has *The Waltz You Saved for Me*. You gotta have a theme song."

Remote broadcasts were just coming in and Bert didn't want to miss the opportunity. "Okay," he said, and sat down at the piano and played three simple chords: *Daah! Daah! DAH!* Then he repeated them: *Daah! Daah DAH!* He was just fooling around, looking for something. Dah! DAH! Dah! DAH! Dah-dah-dah-dah; dah-dah-dah-dah… But in fifteen minutes, starting with those three simple chords and throwing in a handful of quarter-notes, he had written—just in time to go on the air—a little number that became his theme.

Pretty soon, he started to get mail from people who heard the remote and the ones that followed. What was the name of that song? Problem was, it didn't *have* a name, or any lyrics. So he and friends Fred Hamm, Dave Bennett and Chauncey Gray put words to it that were as simple as the melody, and found a publisher. The song was *Bye Bye Blues.*

Bert's timing was perfect. ASCAP, the American Society of Composers, Authors and Publishers founded in 1914, was just starting to carry some weight. That meant royalties on every sheet of music and every recording of his theme, which went on to become a jazz classic recorded by everyone from the Ambrose orchestra to Count Basie to the 1952 version by Les Paul and Mary Ford that reached No. 11 on the US *Hit Parade* show.

It was about that time that I heard the story from Bert Lown himself, sitting in his room at the Hotel Georgia. He was in town attending the Canadian Association of Western Broadcasters convention, long out of the band business and doing public relations and marketing for CBS in Hollywood.

"Dal," he said, "you've got to write a song."

"Why?" I asked.

"Because," he said, "thanks to ASCAP, my royalties on *Bye Bye Blues*, through the Depression, good times and bad, have *never* been less than $5,000 a quarter."

Suddenly, writing a song became a great idea. Lorraine and I worked together on one, came up with a song we called *Love Goes on Forever*, and sent it to Bert in Hollywood. He loved it, even called me at the Roof to tell me so. "I've got the Robbins Corp., a major publishing house," he said. "So, we're set to go."

A month later, he called again. "We're all set," he said. "Hugo Winterhalter's orchestra, Columbia Records, Rosemary Clooney doing the vocal and putting it on her new LP. How's that?"

How *was* it? It was incredible. Clooney and Winterhalter? It couldn't miss.

The recording session goes on as planned. But before a decision can be made on which songs would go on the LP, Bert Lown dies of a heart attack at age fifty-nine. There is no one to stand up for *Love Goes on Forever* when the final cuts are made. Our song winds up on the cutting room floor and never did get a chance to become a hit record.

We were about to begin our first set one Saturday night at the Roof when Lance Harrison opened his saxophone case and discovered that something was missing. No, not his horn. Worse than that. The mickey of gin that made a home there was nowhere to be found.

The band room where we spent intermission was on the sixteenth floor, one floor above the Roof. "Dal," Lance said, "I think I can make it to the liquor store and back. We've got twenty minutes, right?" He turned, ran out of the room, rode the service elevator down to the kitchen, bolted out the service entrance and raced down the lane.

*It only looks like the morning after a wild party. Actually it was a publicity photo for the twentieth anniversary at the Panorama Roof.*

His race was of great interest to the rest of the band. The band room windows overlooked Hornby Street and gave us a great view of his route and of the famous Hornby Street liquor store. We were all pressed to the glass, waiting.

Out came Lance. He ran down the lane to Robson Street, along Robson to Hornby, down Hornby to the liquor store, darted in, made his purchase, raced out, retraced his route back to the hotel, rode the service elevator back up and—*Ta-da!*—made it back just in time to open the next set. One small problem: he was too out of breath to play.

Speaking of running: When we began the Saturday night CBC radio shows from the Roof—which actually started 8:30 p.m. our time to get on the air before the eastern stations shut down for the night—the band had two trumpets. I wanted to add a third to produce a fuller brass sound. The guy I wanted (who wouldn't?) was Bobby Hales, but he was playing with Fraser MacPherson's band at the Cave.

"Do you suppose," I asked, "that Fras would consider timing his intermission so that you could run over here, grab the service elevator to the Roof, sit in with us for half an hour, then run back?"

Bobby was okay with the idea, which meant more bucks in his pocket. He asked Fras, who agreed to try it, and that's what we did for a year.

Herb Capozzi had a theory in his days running the BC Lions. "If you want something spontaneous," he said, "you've got to organize it." I mention this to explain why my saxophone was hidden under my seat at one of Chor Leoni's summer Monday night concerts on the Bard on the Beach stage at Vanier Park in 2005.

Diane Loomer, who founded the now-famous men's choir in 1992, set it up. One number on their program was

*Girl From Ipanema,* the huge hit by Stan Getz featuring the tenor sax solo. Rather than simply have me appear as a guest artist, she announced to the crowd that the sax player in the orchestra just wasn't up to playing the solo in the Getz manner.

"Does anyone know *anybody* we could get who could do it?" she asked. I leaped to my feet and ran down the aisle waving my sax. Diane, feigning great surprise, did a "My gosh, it's *Dal Richards!*" The crowd got a big kick out of it, and we did the number.

When something works that well, you go with it. When we were planning the ninetieth birthday party at the Orpheum and booked Chor Leoni, I huddled with Diane and planned a novel introduction. I introduced Diane, who said she was delighted to be there and then added, "In fact, Dal, there are some other people here to wish you a happy birthday, too." At which point the choir members, scattered through the audience, rose as one and headed for the stage in full, magnificent voice, singing the theme from *A Funny Thing Happened on the Way to the Forum,* a song called *There's Comedy Tonight.* Wonderful thing, spontaneity. Particularly if it comes off the way you planned it.

I was on the horns of a dilemma. My vacation plans were made. My companion at the time, Marilyn Ployart, and I were going to London. Tickets bought, hotel booked, itinerary arranged. But between the planning and the scheduled departure I'd been offered a really lucrative band gig at the Hyatt Regency. I *really* wanted to do that gig. I *really* wanted that London vacation. We'd been planning it for a while. Marilyn might be a tad upset if I called it off.

Desperately, I started checking air line schedules.

Bingo! The flights worked. We could go to London and start the vacation. The morning of the Hyatt gig I could fly back, play the show, grab a couple of hours sleep, rush to the airport, grab a return flight to London and finish the holiday. Mind you, if either flight was delayed…And the timing would be tight enough even if things went smoothly. But it was a prime gig. It was worth a shot.

Marilyn and I went to London. On gig day I awakened early, streaked to the airport, caught the flight home, grabbed a taxi, roared to my apartment, picked up my horns and tux, and headed for the Hyatt, where Bud Henderson, as he'd promised, had the band ready to go. The show went well, I think. Don't remember much of it. The instant it ended I was hailing a taxi for home. In the morning I was back at the airport boarding another flight to London. As I recall, I arrived on time, but for a couple of days I was a little bit goofy from jet lag.

# A Little Marching Music

*"I sit here in my office right next to the stage and there have been a million things to look after, a million things happening. But when I hear the first downbeat from Dal and the band on opening day, I know everything is going to be fine."*

Mike McDaniel, PNE President and CEO.

W e go back a ways, the Pacific National Exhibition and I. About seventy-eight years, give or take. In fact, it wasn't even called the PNE, it was the Vancouver Industrial Exhibition that night in the early '30s when I discovered that if you stood on tiptoe outside the window of the Happyland Ballroom you could see the Ronnie Hart orchestra and hear Ronnie sing his theme song, *One Hour with You*, with his little speech at the finish about how he'd like to spend one hour with—finger pointed to the audience—*you*.

I was just a kid in love with the music and willing to go anywhere to hear it. Even the midway barker who put me in the straitjacket couldn't dim that.

It's my earliest Fair recollection. I was about seven years old, walking along the midway with my father. We got separated. I must have looked confused because a barker fronting one of the shows came down off his stage, took my hand and took me onstage with him.

"Put out your hands," he said. I did, and he pulled out a straitjacket and put it on me. Just about then my father located me and came bounding up the stairs. I wasn't distressed, but my dad certainly was. Who knew that one day people at the PNE would sit on a bench inscribed "In celebration of 65 years of entertainment provided by Dal Richards and his Orchestra. August 4, 2004."

It's seventy years now. We've got the band in the open-air theatre and the crowds still come out, so I hope to be there every year for as long as I can stand up and blow. And the good thing is, I don't have to wear lederhosen. I did more than once in the days when the PNE had a lot of bands—rube bands (as in "Hey, Rube!", the old circus cry that rang out when the local yokels caused trouble), concert bands, marching bands giving it the old oom-pa-pa in lederhosen. I'd started out in 1938 when Mr. D invited me to join his marching band for the opening day PNE parade. It got pretty gruelling—and boring—marching for four or five hours, especially on those hot summer days. We'd start on Georgia Street four or five blocks west of Burrard, turn on Burrard down to Hastings and out Hastings to Clark Drive, where the march ended—fortuitously at a corner in front of a beer

*The PNE had a lot of marching bands, including this one featuring lederhosen-clad musicians (that's me, top right) giving it the old oom-pa-pa.*

parlour. Made a man grateful to be playing the clarinet or sax. I always felt kind of sorry for the guys toting the tubas.

It was with the outdoor band that we came into our own. I'd been out there since the '60s. We were the pit band for the Startime shows at Empire Stadium, which pulled in the big acts for the big crowds: Rosemary Clooney, Bobby Darin, Nelson Eddy, the King Sisters, Frank Sinatra Jr....They had their run, but died when rains kept coming, drenching the high-priced talent and those customers not fortunate enough to have seats under cover. So we moved into the Coliseum for a few years of afternoon dances where my band alternated with Mart Kenney's. When Bobby Hales got the PNE music concession we played various bandstands under his coordination. We also played for the Miss PNE contests until political correctness squashed that.

*Even Arthur Delamont could not have envisioned the staying power of the Kitsilano Boys Band he organized in 1929. But there we were in 2004 celebrating the band's seventy-fifth anniversary at the Kitsilano Showboat.*

But times were changing. Dance music was no longer enough. We'd worked toward becoming a show band, which we are totally now. Once we had played one outdoor season, the PNE brass recognized that we were pulling people through the gates and on to the grounds. After a lot of years, we were the feature band.

It wasn't always peaceful on the PNE grounds. Take the day in 1980 that the PNE took on Mr. D.

I'd been playing with his professional band as lots of Kits band grads did, and that included some highly qualified talent. We'd played at English Bay, at Malkin Bowl, and now Mr. D, hearing the Parks Board concerts had been dropped, applied to play a concert with the ex-Kits group on the PNE grounds. "Sorry," he was told. "No room on the program."

It was like waving a red flag.

"Really," said Mr. D. "Well, I guess the only other choice for me is to bring my boys just outside the grounds and play behind a big sign saying we've been refused a spot on the program. I'll pay them myself."

They found a spot on the program.

And then there was the night of June 9, 2004, at a hot-and-heavy meeting of Vancouver city council, with public input invited, on the thorny issue of whether to leave the PNE where it was or move it somewhere else. Nearby residents wanted it somewhere else—anywhere else. Both sides jammed the meeting to be heard.

In his column in the next day's *Vancouver Sun*, Pete McMartin covered it this way:

## DAL RICHARDS BRINGS "LOVE"
## TO PNE BATTLEGROUND

On Monday night, at the ungodly hour of 9:30 p.m., Mayor Larry Campbell looked down at his list of 111 speakers wishing to address Vancouver city council on the future of the PNE, and called out: "Dal Richards?"

Dal Richards, 86-year-old citizen, orchestra leader and Vancouver landmark, strode to the podium. He looked good, natty in a tan jacket set off by a matching tie and pocket hankie. He smiled at the council members, thanked them and said, deadpan:

"I feel a very close link to the PNE, you know, because from time to time I've been referred to as a heritage institution also." The crowd in the packed council chambers laughed. Campbell grinned and sat back in his chair—a small gesture of deference, as if to say, "Dal, the floor's yours." Up until then, Campbell had enforced a strict five-minute limit for speakers to make their case, but Campbell looked like he would let Richards have all the time he wanted.

And then Richards, by way of introduction, said he had not come tonight to speak to council so much about the shape of the PNE, or about the future of the PNE, but about the "aesthetics" of the PNE. He said:

"People will forget what you did, and people will forget what you said, but people will never forget how you made them feel."

He then said he had performed at the PNE for 65 consecutive years—a humbling number a few people in the crowd whistled at in amazement.

In those 65 years, Richards said, the one constant he experienced was the people who would come up to him at the foot of the bandstand "and tell me about their memories of the PNE"—of dancing to Harry James, or of meeting their future spouse there for the first time, or of spending a summer evening that, 40 and 50 and 60 years later, was still perfect and perfectly remembered. Then Richards said:

"Heritage is not only marked by design and buildings and architecture—it's love, and the ties to things around us marked by that love."

It was odd to hear that word in the council chambers, and you could feel the crowd turn to it. "Love" had not come up before. "Love" had not been included in any of the four options that staff had presented to council for the future design of the PNE. Up until then, the speakers had talked about greening and job creation and horse barns and Playland and water supply, and some had even talked about tradition and a fondness for simple pleasures. But no one had talked about love. And many people loved the PNE, Richards said, because it was the one place where so many of us over so many years had gone with our loved ones to have some fun.

Richards then told a story about another Vancouver landmark that had been threatened with redevelopment:

Thirty years ago, he said, the Orpheum Theatre was on the verge of destruction, only to be saved by impresario Hugh Pickett and then-Vancouver-mayor Art Phillips, who decided, by means of a benefit performance, to start a fund-raising campaign to save the Orpheum.

He himself had loved the Orpheum, Richards said, because it was a place where he had learned a great lesson as an entertainer.

It was in the spring of 1940, on a Friday night, and Richards had been booked by manager Ivan Ackery to play in between shows. He was 22, Richards said, and "full of himself," and after the show, which went well, he was backstage with Ackery "looking for a compliment."

"And Ackery said, 'Good show, Dal, but you forgot the balcony ... you didn't play to the people in the balcony.'"

That is, Richards was saying, he was so full of himself he had played to the swells in the high-priced seats, the ones he could see and most wanted to win approval from, but he had forgotten all those unseen faces up in the nosebleed territory, who deserved just as much of his respect and heeding.

"I had looked out at the people in the audience," Richards said, "but forgotten about the people up in the balcony."

Richards, with a musician's timing, paused a quarter-note to let the idea sink in. Then he said:

"So I urge you, ladies and gentlemen, don't forget the people in the balcony."

The applause was loud and sustained. Overhead, the people in the front row of the balcony were leaning over the edge and clapping. Richards stepped away from the podium. As he was leaving, Campbell, leaning into his microphone, said:

"Dal, as always, you were right on the money. Five minutes exactly."

I don't know how much I had to do with it, if anything, but the PNE stayed where it was, and is. For which we can all be grateful.

*Riding in style as the grand marshal in the 2008 PNE parade.*

# Intermission

*"If I have to drag you by the ass I'm going to get you through these Christmas exams!"*

Frank Gruen, statistics instructor, BCIT.

I was hauling my horns, PA system and music stands up the stairs to the second floor of the Boilermaker's Hall on Pender Street for a New Year's Eve gig in 1965, carrying it all myself because hiring a roadie would cost money I'd rather see go to the band, when it hit me. I sat down on a stair and faced reality: the big band business was on life support. It was time to find another line of work.

A year earlier I'd played New Year's Eve at the Roof as I'd done for twenty-five years. The coast-to-coast CBC *Dance Parade* radio broadcast had bounced from hotel to hotel across the country—Halifax to Montreal to Toronto to Winnipeg to Edmonton to Vancouver, where we broadcast the final segment. The good life, it seemed, was going to go on forever. Now I was going to work a dance at the Boilermaker's Hall because it was the only gig I could get.

We'd been let go at the Roof in late July. It had caught me totally by surprise. There hadn't been so much as a hint.

Now the scramble began, bands from all over the city battling over employment scraps. The jobs weren't there. A kid named Elvis and four British mopheads called the Beatles had seen to that. Between them, they and their imitators blanketed the charts. Nobody remembered what a big band was.

I hit the streets like everyone else, looking for any sort of gig. I'd phone home to ask Lorraine if there were any calls. There never were. "Are you *sure?*" I'd ask. Her answer never changed. Maybe it never would. Time to quit hoping and get working.

I examined my qualifications for a line of employment that didn't involve blowing a clarinet or saxophone. There weren't a lot, but I had an idea. I'd spent a lot of time in a lot of hotels. I knew about band bookings. I'd been on the employee end of a lot of them. Maybe if I was educated in the finer points of the business end I might be of some use in the hotel business. After thirty years or so out in the big bad world, it was time to go back to school.

The BC Institute of Technology was offering a hotel management course. I went out for an interview. They were very encouraging, but thought that thirty-year absentee record might make things difficult. Still, after several talks with the principal, Gordon Thom, I enrolled in the fall of '66. Fine, but there was still a small matter of making a living. I wasn't broke. I'd done some investing when the money was coming in. I knew there was enough put aside to make the two-year school term manageable. We'd given up our large Kerrisdale home and moved into an apartment. We'd get by. But Dallas was at UBC. Lorraine was at home. Being a full-time student wouldn't work.

Then, in November, I got a chance to put a five-piece combo in the Holiday Inn on Helmcken and Howe streets, six nights a week, 9 p.m. to 1 a.m. Things got a little tricky, what with classes starting at 8:30 a.m. and a lot of homework. I hadn't been up before 10:30 a.m. in forty years. To add to the work load, the 1966 Grey Cup game was being held in Vancouver and CFL commissioner G. Sydney Halter had signed me to direct the halftime show. I felt like a one-armed juggler. Without a couple of teachers who went above and beyond the call of duty, I might never have made it.

I'd devised all sorts of trickery to keep all the balls in the air. I'd phone home on the noon break for business calls, but there were only a couple of pay phones and I didn't always beat the rush to get to one before everyone else on break started calling their girl- or boyfriends. I needed to make those calls. Victor Heath, head of the Forestry Department, saw my problem and stepped in. "I'm not using my office in the noon hour. I'm away at lunch. Here's a key. Go in, make yourself comfortable, and make your calls." On call-free noon hours, the school nurse let me grab catnaps on the cot in the infirmary.

Heading into Christmas I was still playing six nights a week. Exams were imminent and I hadn't written one for years. My particular nemesis was mathematics and statistics. I'd had nothing to do with math except for making out band payrolls. But one night our teacher, Frank Gruen, showed up at the hotel, where I had a room and was doing my assignments on breaks.

"Let's get to it," he said, and started to show me how to do the math, in effect teaching an extra, private class. It was

*At age 48, 30 years out of Magee High, the big band business no longer viable, I was back in school, taking a hotel management course at the BC Institute of Technology, once again facing the perils of homework.*

almost Christmas. He had a family. But there he was at the club, on more than one occasion, helping me. One night, I asked him why.

He grabbed me by the lapels of my tux.

"Richards," he began, "you're the oldest guy on campus..."

(Well, he was right about that. I was so much older than anyone else I found out later that at first most of them thought I was an instructor, then decided I was too old to be one. Apparently my nickname was Boss Baby, and it wasn't until they saw me leading the band at a school concert out on the cafeteria patio that they realized I was a musician.) "And if I have to drag you by the ass I'm going to get you through these exams!"

Exam time arrived, and I took every second of every minute allotted to write every test, checking and rechecking in the hope of bleeding out one more mark. (Years later, Peter Woolley, who'd marked the accounting papers, was a guest at the UBC Opera Society ball at the Chan Centre and recalled that he'd been highly impressed because the test had contained a complex, progressive question that had to be solved in a series of steps, and I was one of the few who nailed it.) And, with the confidence those first-semester marks had instilled, I was much more comfortable the rest of the way—so much so that when I graduated from the two-year course I was given the BC and Yukon Hotels Association's award for achieving the highest standing in class.

Speaking of confidence, after those first Christmas exams I felt so good I made another deal. The Commodore was holding public dances on Saturday nights now in addition to the private parties during the week. I was still playing at the Holiday Inn, but I approached Doug Gourlay, then owner of the Commodore, offering my band for the Saturday affairs. He said yes, and my Saturdays got hectic. I'd play a few numbers at the Inn, take a break, rush out the back door, run down the alley to the Commodore where Bud Henderson, my long-time pianist and friend, was standing in as my band leader, jump on the stage, play a few numbers, sing a couple of songs, then rush back to the Inn in time for the final set. Crazy? Probably. But it was a few more bucks in the bank. School kids like me needed them. Besides, I had fond memories of the Commodore that stretched clear back to my final year in high school.

My band was popular with Magee students, but not so much with principal Alan Bowles, who had nothing against me but was very much against dance and jazz bands playing at noon pep rallies. He thought it agitated students and might cause them to return to class with their minds not on their studies but on things more capricious.

I produced the school concert for three years, along with guitarist Wally Peters and Bernie Braden, a singer who would go on to great success in Toronto and later in London with his wife, Barbara Kelly. (Bernie and I actually did a fifteen-minute show on CJOR on which I played tenor sax and he sang. We got $5 to split. We thought it was pretty good.) Following one of our concerts, Wally and I were back in Mr. Osterhout's mathematics class, where he complimented us on its success, then added "But it would be nice if you could do a little mathematics, too." We took the hint.

The next concert was coming up, and the school auditorium was rather shabby. I wanted a picture taken of me and my band, but the backdrop just didn't cut it. So, no doubt emboldened by Bensted's and my success conning our way into ballrooms on the Kits band trips, I called the Commodore, spoke to Don Flynn, the band leader in those days, and asked him if it would be all right if I brought my high school band down and had the picture taken in the

Commodore. (Hey, all he could say was no.) But Flynn was amused by the idea, got permission from management, and made it happen.

My education gamble had paid off. Right after graduation in June of 1968, I landed a job as Director of Conventions and Conferences at the University of British Columbia. Translation: try to fill the vacated students' residences with conference attendees to increase the revenue from that department and pay off the mortgage of the new ones being built at the time. I devised a scheme that worked out pretty well.

Over the years at the Roof I'd become friends with Grant McConachie of Canadian Pacific Airlines. Grant and his wife were regulars at the club. In fact, Lorraine and I were the beneficiaries of a couple of free flights to Mexico. Through Grant, I set up a package with CPA's director of sales and marketing that saw students from Tokyo or other large Japanese cities fly to Vancouver via CPA for a four-week ESL (English as a second language) course in residence at UBC followed by a week at the Banff Hot Springs Hotel (because the first word Japanese think of when they hear "Canada" is "Rockies"). It was a big success and was still operating when I left UBC two years later.

One of my other successful programs was to get the BC Lions football team to hold training camp at UBC—staying, of course, in the residences. It was a good fit. UBC had lots of fields and having the camp in town made it easier for all the local media to come out, as opposed to the out-of-town

*In 1956, year two of the BC Lions' existence, I became the leader of the band that performed pre-game and halftime shows at Empire Stadium. Here I am with the team's very first mascot, the acrobatic Mary Stewart.*

camps where only the big papers and TV stations sent people on the road for the entire two weeks. My club contact was Bob Ackles, then director of player development, who would go on to become a CFL legend and return in 2002 after a long and successful stint in the National Football League to rebuild a tottering Lions' franchise. I kept an eye on things and made sure I never neglected my major assignment: to keep coach Jackie Parker's fridge stocked with Beefeater gin.

Of course, I had an edge in dealing with the Lions.

About a week before their first-season opener I got a phone call. The Canadian Football League had decided the team needed a fight song, something to put some pizzazz into the official opening ceremonies. Could I help? I got together with a lady named Peggy Miller and several club directors at the Arctic Club. Peggy had written a set of lyrics.

I read them and thought they'd work with something the band played regularly, an old tune called *I Love the Sunshine of Your Smile* that was the theme of a British band leader named Billy Cotton—whom I'd actually seen during the London tour with the Kits band.

*Love the Sunshine of Your Smile* became *C'mon And Roar, You Lions, Roar.* Thanks to Peggy, the song and the new lyrics seemed made for each other:

> C'mon and roar, you Lions, roar,
> That's what a Lion's roar is for.
> From the mountains to the sea,
> You are the pride of all BC!
> (RAH! RAH! RAH!)
> So buckle up and play the game!
> And lead us all to football fame!
> We love the L, the I, the O-N-S,
> C'mon and roar, you Lions,
> Roar you Lions!
> Roar you Lions, roar!
> (RAH! RAH! RAH!)

I don't know if Billy Cotton would have been pleased at what we'd done to his theme song, but we thought it was great. The fans loved it—still do—and for thirty seasons I marched down the Empire Stadium field, resplendent in orange suit and white straw hat, conducting Gordon Olson's Beefeater marching band, my forty-piece Lions' house band and fifty cheerleaders doing routines choreographed by Grace Macdonald. The term "conducting" is used in its loosest sense. It was march music, all one tempo, but I was marching in front of the band. I figured I had to be doing *something*, so I waved my arm back and forth like a windshield wiper.

The 1979 version of the BC Lions' band in one of its rare sit-down moments, posing for a shot at Empire Stadium. Dill Cunningham photo

Funny, the way things work out. At one BC Lions' game as I was waiting with my band to march onto the field who should I see but Scott Ackles, Bob's son, there to give me my cue. "Okay, Mr. Richards," he said. "Time to march on." Scott was working with the Lions, learning the business. Today he's the president of the Calgary Stampeders and in 2008 got to hoist the Grey Cup for the Stamps as his dad had done with the Lions. He is also a dedicated and knowledgable blues fan who can find the best clubs any place he happens to be. But I can still hear him.

*"Okay, Mr. Richards. Time to march on..."*

The Lions were big on halftime entertainment in those early years, particularly their first coach, Annis Stukus, whose approach was pure pragmatism: "There isn't gonna be much winning done around here for the first few years," he said. The '54 British Empire Games—bid for and won by Vancouver partially as an excuse to get funding and erect Empire Stadium so the city could get a pro football franchise, were barely over before the Lions launched their first season, so the Games band led by Arthur Delamont carried on with the Lions. I was a member that year and took over leadership in the second year.

Halftime was a different story. The Lions wanted a marching band, but no one had any idea how to handle the intricate marching and staging. So, for about ten years, they imported high school marching bands from Bellingham and later from Ferndale. Then came the Beefeaters. Now we had two bands totalling about 120 musicians, and began to have choreographed shows using Vancouver talent with the marching bands in between acts. The challenge was to find different routines and themes so the home crowds saw a different show each game.

By then, Herb Capozzi was the Lions' general manager and with Herb cost was never a matter of concern. Gordon, Grace and I would lay out the show, I'd go into Herb's office and explain what we'd planned and he'd ask only one question: "Will it work?" I once briefly considered arriving in front of the band by parachute. Herb didn't even blink.

Then one day I had the idea of staging the world's largest sing-along, hopefully with a sellout crowd of thirty thousand or so. Great idea! We had slides made up with

*Annis Stukus, first head coach of the BC Lions, had a theory: If the team isn't going to be good, make sure the entertainment is. The Beefeaters' band more than did their part.*

the words to all the songs and constructed a huge screen that would slide over the scoreboard at the north end of the stadium on which the projectionist, who'd climbed up a specially constructed scaffold tower, would flash the words, verse by verse.

We had the two bands, majorettes and various local singers split into circles of about a hundred each. Rehearsal was flawless. Then came halftime. The screen was dropped over the scoreboard, the lights dimmed. That's when we discovered the plan's major flaw.

The rehearsal had been held at 5 p.m. in the empty stadium. Come game time, the scaffold tower was surrounded by kids from the Woodward's Quarterback

Club. When they saw the projectionist climbing the tower with his load of slides they had to know what was going on. Naturally, they also had to shake the tower, which caused the carefully stacked slides of the lyrics to spill all over the place.

The projectionist was still trying to get them re-sorted when the bands began to play and the fans broke into song. The man tried mightily, holding a slide up to the light to read the lyrics, popping it into the projector and looking at another slide. It was a lost cause. Soon the lyrics he was flashing had little if anything to do with the music we were playing. "This," I thought, "can only get worse." Then we got a break. We were playing *Show Me the Way to Go Home/I'm tired and I wanna go to bed*. I'm not sure what the projectionist was flashing. But when we got to the line *I had a little drink about an hour ago* the audience burst out laughing and somehow the experiment wound up a big success.

That's the only downside of live performance: you never know when or how something is going to screw up your carefully laid plans. Take the Miss Grey Cup pageant in Vancouver in 1974 in the ballroom of the Westin Bayshore.

The way it was supposed to work, contestants representing the nine Canadian Football League teams would parade out individually on a runway from the stage while we played their team's fight song. When the winner was chosen and named she would go back up the runway to the stage to her team's song while she was announced as Miss Grey Cup 1974.

But as she began that walk, the kitchen doors were flung open and out raced this person in runners and tennis shorts carrying a tennis racquet who leaped up onto the runway with the winner. No one knew who he was or what he was doing there. These days security guards might have jumped him or worse. But no one knew what was going on, so there he stood.

As it turned out it was Bobby Riggs, the well-known tennis hustler. A year earlier, Riggs had turned a few calculatedly disparaging remarks about the inferiority of the women's pro tennis tour into a big-money showdown with Margaret Court, who was so psyched he won easily, and then had an even bigger payday as Billie Jean King challenged and took him apart. Now he was in Vancouver on some sort of promotion (including a ping-pong game with the Lions' Jimmy "Dirty 30" Young, in which Young used a ping-pong paddle and Riggs used a frying pan). The Miss Grey Cup pageant was on national TV. The ham in him couldn't resist and the stunt got worldwide TV exposure.

Speaking of television exposure, a bandleader friend of mine named Del Courtney, who played at the St. Francis Hotel in San Francisco and, in the summer months, at the Royal Hawaiian in Honolulu, was also in charge of the halftime shows for the NFL's Oakland Raiders. He knew about our own halftime productions at Empire Stadium and suggested we bring Gordon Olson's Beefeaters band to Oakland to provide the halftime show at a nationally televised Raiders' home game. The band bused to Oakland. I produced the show and the US crowd heard *Roar, You*

*Lions, Roar.* It was a thrill for the band members and a notable occasion for all of us.

In 1964, it was the cheerleaders' turn to draw media attention. The Lions, beaten by the Hamilton Tiger-Cats at home in the Grey Cup final the year before, were in Toronto for another shot at the title and a little revenge. The Lions' cheerleaders came in by train. I'd flown down and was in the Royal York hotel lobby with Grace McDonald, who was about to cross the street to Union Station to meet them. I had an idea. Instead of merely walking across the street in civvies, Grace had the girls don their uniforms and *march* across Front Street, single file. The jaunt took the fifty of them five minutes. They stopped traffic, flashbulbs popped, and story and pictures appeared across Canada. To make it

*Quarterback Joe Kapp (l) and running back Willie Fleming, heroes of the '64 Grey Cup victory, were back in Vancouver for a visit in 1975—and found themselves as popular as ever.*

even sweeter, the Lions finished the weekend with their first Grey Cup victory.

In November, 2004, there was a final chapter to the *Roar, You Lions* story. The Lions' fight song hadn't been played for a few years, replaced by PA system rock, volume just over the threshold of pain. A bunch of guys were sitting around Paul Airey's Sound Kitchen studio (where I tape *Dal's Place*, my radio show on AM650) and decided to do a new version. Bob Ackles, the Lions' GM, was all for it, and it was done using the version I'd recorded in Toronto with members of the Spitfire Band and the Laurie Bower Singers in 1968. (Trivia question: Who played glockenspiel? Answer: Peter Appleyard.)

Came a phone call to Paul Airey at the Sound Kitchen from the Lions' office: "Is the guy who wrote the original song still around? Do you think we could bring him to centre field and honour him? How old is he?"

"Late '80s," Paul said.

"Oh," she said, doubtfully. "Well, do you think you could get him out to centre field?"

"He'll jog out," Paul said.

"But, it's sixty yards!"

"He'll jog out," Paul repeated.

At halftime on game night they introduced me. I jogged out. Ackles knew I would. He'd seen me swim a couple hundred yards. The young kids on his staff didn't believe it. They actually had plans to wheel me out. Sorry, kids.

The following year my name was added to the Lions' Wall of Fame in the builder category.

—— ❖ ——

*You can't have a football team without cheerleaders, and the BC "Fe-Lions" add beauty and dance routines to the Lions' home games at BC Place.*

The UBC experience was invaluable but in terms of making a career in the hotel management business it had its limits. One night when we were doing a gig at the Bayshore I heard that the owner of the International Jet Inn near the Seatac airport in Seattle was in the audience. During a break I introduced myself and, sensing that there might be job possibilities, later sent him my resume. He was very impressed by my qualifications as a graduate of BCIT's hospitality program, and offered me a position of assistant manager of the hotel, which would mean managing and booking talent for the new lounge he was about to open. The idea rather appealed to me, but there was an immediate problem: I needed a work permit, and my efforts to get one ricocheted me from US Immigration to labour hall and back to Immigration. I was getting nowhere until one of the Immigration officers noticed my name and something twigged.

"Dal Richards," he said. "I've heard that name before. I heard your band when I was stationed in Blaine. You guys are pretty good!"

Down came the stamp. Slam! I had my permit.

There was another potential problem. Under Washington state labour laws jobs had to be posted in various cities. Any city with a population of 25,000 or greater had a labour office where candidates had to list their qualifications and compete for the position. On that score I wasn't too worried. On my list I included my BCIT graduation with honours with hotel management experience *and* the fact that I was a musician. How many other candidates would have that combined skill set? I got the job.

I liked Seattle and, in particular, the way Americans did business: none of that "I'll have to check with the boss" stuff response to sales calls. You got your answer in one call. But much of my market still was in Vancouver. I'd live in Seattle for five days, then come home on weekends or sometimes earlier to contact travel agents who had clients wanting a short jaunt to Seattle or those who used the city as a stop-off point on their way to Hawaii. I set up a package: one night's accommodation and free car parking for two weeks for the Hawaii-bounds. It was a good deal and for me it had a side benefit. The hotel owner lived in Portland but would come to Seattle every few weeks to check on business. When he saw the lot with all those cars with BC plates, I was gold.

Seattle holds fond memories for me, starting back in the Kits band days even before the Chicago World's Fair trip. The Greater Vancouver Tourist Association invited the band to participate in a pre-Christmas show designed to generate interest in tourist trips to BC. We stayed at the YMCA, but Bensted and I found our way to the Olympic Hotel in search of big band music and found, to our delight, that a balcony ran all around the lobby, and at the north end it overlooked the Georgian Room where Dick Jurgens' orchestra was in full swing. We'd heard Jurgens and his trademark "Here's that *band* again!" intro on Seattle's KJR radio. So we parked in the balcony and listened the night away—a forerunner, you might say, to the ploy we later used in hotels in Chicago and London.

During my stay at the Jet Inn I got to know the Seattle-Tacoma airport very well, negotiating contracts with airlines to have their crews—pilots, stewardesses, stewards—stay at the Jet, and they could be interesting guests from a management standpoint. I even did one band gig at the Olympic, hiring some Seattle musicians for a combo to play a social function held by a Seattle travel agent. All in all, a great time, but after a year I decided it was time to come home. So when well-known local entrepreneur and philanthropist Roy Lisogar built and opened a new hotel called the Century Plaza in 1972 I made a pitch to become his director of sales and marketing. Not only did Roy give me the job, but come Christmas he gave me a $500 bonus— to this day the only Christmas bonus I've ever received.

It was an interesting introduction to a new career because, due to a nationwide strike by the Otis Elevator Company, both the Century Plaza and the new Hyatt Regency hotel were completed without elevators. Since the Plaza had thirty storeys and the Hyatt thirty-four, renting rooms on the upper levels required a degree of salesmanship. What we did was set one rate for floors one to five, a lower rate for floors five to ten. The better stair-climber you were, the better rate you got. If your heart and legs could stand it and you had plenty of time, you could get a hell of a deal on a 30th-floor suite, but I don't remember ever renting one.

I couldn't have asked for a better boss than Roy Lisogar, which was why I had to give it a lot of thought when I got a call in 1974 from Ken Evans, assistant to Hotel Georgia manager John Egan, asking if I'd be interested in coming to the Georgia as director of sales. The Georgia was in the heart of the city. It had a wonderful history. I'd played there with the Kitsilano Boys Band in those Sunday afternoon concerts sponsored by Safeway and broadcast on CKWX. Roy, ever supportive in my fledgling hotel career, gave the move his blessing and off I went. That same year, I devised what you might call the Lawrence Welk caper.

I'd made a kind of connection with Lawrence during my tenure at the Century Plaza. The advance man for his upcoming appearance at Pacific Coliseum came in to book rooms for the stay. We discussed it over lunch, he used my office for the day, provided a couple of tickets for the show and introduced me to Lawrence, who presented me with a baton engraved with his name. To be honest, I had no idea of the popularity he and his band enjoyed—the show was a total sellout—but before it was over I made certain the advance man had my card and was aware of my impending move to the Hotel Georgia. When the Welk show came back to town, they stayed at the Georgia.

Recalling that previous sellout, I went to the show's sponsors and, not without a sense of trepidation, reserved two hundred tickets. Now all I had to do was get two hundred occupants into the Georgia to use them. I contacted a friend who owned a travel agency in Victoria and proposed a round-trip bus and ferry trip package to include a room at the hotel, tickets to the show and breakfast the morning after.

The response was staggering. Before long I was after the sponsor for more tickets, then asking again for another batch. I sold out the Georgia, shifted some of the purchasers to the Ritz Hotel, sold that out; did the same at the Devonshire and a motel on Howe Street. And there was a bonus.

I'd asked the advance man if it would be possible to have Mr. Welk make an appearance at the breakfast along with the Welk stars who had agreed to attend. I'd made no promises, but had told my friend at the travel agency that I'd give it a shot. The best the advance man could do was suggest that I ask Mr. Welk myself when he arrived. I went to the airport to pick up this man who'd become one of the best-known and arguably most popular bandleaders in the land. We talked music business all the way in and he graciously agreed to appear at the brunch. My indebtedness to him has been heartfelt ever since.

One of the huge perks of working at the Georgia was that the hotel was part of an arrangement known as the Preferred Hotels Reservation System, in which the sales

*There have been many great and famous bandleaders, but in terms of sheer popularity Lawrence Welk would be high on anyone's list and on top of a lot of them. In his two '70s appearances in Vancouver, he truly was "wunnerful, wunnerful."*

directors of some of the finest hotels in North America would meet about once a year in one city or another, discuss the business, and receive information and contact numbers from the director in the host city regarding people whose companies' employees travelled around the continent and might be convinced to stop off in one of the Preferred Hotels should their travels take them to that city.

Naturally, the sales director of the host city wanted his hotel to make a good impression on the other directors, so they made certain that the visiting members stayed in only the finest suites the hotel could offer. That, in turn, meant that when I travelled to the meetings, I rattled around in luxury suites in the Stanford Court in San Francisco, the Watergate and Embassy Suites in Washington, the Congress in Chicago, the Warwick in Houston, the Century Plaza in Los Angeles, the Pierre in New York City, the Ponchartrain in New Orleans…

A guy could get used to that sort of lifestyle, particularly when the cities in which you were staying, and often the hotels themselves, provided opportunities to hear some great bands after I had finished my hotel business. But it was all coming to an end. In 1979, Nelson and Eleni Skalbania, who were running the Hotel Devonshire, bought the Hotel Georgia. With the two hotels side by side, Eleni decided to put both operations under one management. Among the immediate casualties, the Georgia Coffee Shop, something of a Vancouver institution, albeit a losing proposition. The employee casualty list was long and disheartening. One of the names on it was Dal Richards, director of sales.

Once again, I needed a job, and found one at the Hotel Devonshire, which, as the dust settled on the Skalbanias' purchase of the Georgia, was now owned by Ron Schon. But there was a twist: the hotel was already earmarked for demolition in two years.

Anyone who's been through both phases will tell you that closing a hotel is even more difficult than getting one open. The employees, some of them, stop caring. As Demolition Day approached, things began to disappear. One day a picture would be hanging on a wall where it had hung for years, the next day you'd see only the outline. But as sales director it was still my job to entice people into the building, and preferably book a room for more than a blissful afternoon. One of our gimmicks: a Last Chance special. Anyone who'd honeymooned at the hotel at any time could spend two days and two nights there at their original rate. One couple got the best suite in the place for $12.

I also brought in a kilted, bearded bartender/singer and his trio, Robert Stuart and the Republicans, who'd built a big following playing Thursday through Saturday at the Georgia's King George V Pub. He'd get the crowd going with the trio, then offer a drink to his friends in the entertainment business to come up and sing or play. Lance Harrison was a frequent performer, and I'd sometimes haul out my tenor sax and jam with him. Unfortunately, his system had a major flaw. His band and the outside entertainment it attracted became so popular that people would fill the place, buy one beer, and nurse it through the evening while they listened to the music.

But he was an attraction, and we needed one. So I put him in the Dev's pub, the Elbow Room. Things went pretty well, until I noticed that so many of his friends/performers were getting free drinks it was cutting into the profits.

One night I called him in to discuss it, the month's bar tab list in my hand.

"Let me see that list," he said, and started to read them off:

"Two Beefeaters. That would be you and Lance.

"Two Beefeaters. You and Lance.

"Two Beefeaters. You and Lance. Two…"

"Never mind," I said. He'd made his point.

It was around about that time that I quit drinking for good. I'd never been a drunk or anything close to it, but at the Georgia when the Howe Street rounders came in for lunch, especially on Fridays after the markets closed, I'd buy a round and it was mid-afternoon before we knew it. It was a public relations thing I had to do, but I came to the conclusion that, aside from anything else, it was time wasting and getting in the way. So one day I quit. Just like that. Cold turkey. From then on when I drank with the boys the bartenders knew that when I ordered a cold Black Russian it meant diet Coke, and a hot Black Russian meant coffee. Incidentally, the day I quit drinking, I also quit smoking. It was a long day.

*When the Hotel Devonshire closed in 1981, broadcaster Earl "The Pearl" Bradford was there to record my final thoughts on the historic building, which was imploded a few days later.* Dave Peterson photo, the *Province*

The Dev was imploded in 1981. I moved on to the Skyline Hotel for about a year as sales manager while simultaneously booking acts like Buddy Greco, whom my band backed, in the Ritz Cabaret, which was in a separate building, along with two banquet rooms, about fifty yards west of the hotel. Burton Cummings, a buddy of the owner's son, rehearsed the Guess Who there for about a month before launching the group's reunion tour. But, although I didn't realize it at the time, my stay at the Devonshire was a turning point. There was a ballroom over the Devonshire's Seafood House that wasn't getting much use. I started holding Saturday night dances there, which became so popular I booked the band for a recording date at Pinewood Studios in 1982, and cut an LP: *Swing is In… Let's Dance!* The tunes were the same stuff I'd been playing all my life, but darned if it didn't catch on. Radio stations gave it air time. Reviews were good: *"This album is good news for those who enjoy dancing to a smooth jazz-oriented big band,"* said the Ottawa *Citizen*'s jazz reviewer. On the CBC's *Disc Drive* show, Jurgen Gothe told listeners: *"I'm not old enough to claim this music is rightful, sweaty palms, falling in love at the prom heritage, but damn it's good."* I was being interviewed again. The album was such a hit that a year later we went back to Pinewood and cut another one, called, cleverly enough, *Swing is In…Vol II.*

They were a treat to do, a gathering of some of the finest musicians in the city and, for that matter, in the country. Bud Henderson on piano; Stan Johnson on bass; Blaine Wikjord on drums; a sax section with Cliff Binion and me on alto, Lance Harrison and Wally Snider on tenor and

*In 1982, gambling on what we saw as the stirrings of a big band revival, we recorded an LP,* Swing Is In...Let's Dance! *The response was so positive we cut another Volume II a year later. Our hunch had been good: our music was back.* Bill Cunningham photo

Don Dorazio on baritone; Stu Barnett, Don Clark and Jamie Croil on trumpet; Dave Robbins, Ed Cowan and Jack Fulton on trombone. On *Vol II*, Carse Sneddon joined the trumpet section and Lew Hilton played baritone sax.

It was a great reunion with arrangements by Lance, Eddie Graf, Harry Boone and Dave Robbins. And the best part— we knew by the response that our music had survived the Beatles, survived Elvis, survived all the other fans and fancies that had seemed to bury it. The icing came in 1995 when the Roof, which had been operating with a combo supplying the music, was finally closing. A final Saturday farewell was planned, and our band was hired for the gig. I knew that, with all of the Roof's history, one night would never be enough for all the people who'd want to say a last goodbye. I suggested that they sell tickets for Saturday and add a Friday show if it sold out. "You're going to have a lot of old Roof patrons upset if they can't get in," I warned. They agreed to add a Friday night show if Saturday sold out, then a Thursday night show if Friday night sold out. We wound up doing five nights. We were back in business.

I was a full-time bandleader again—but I wasn't the same guy who'd sat on those stairs at the Boilermaker's Hall back in 1965 wondering what to do with his life. The

*What better way to plug a new release than to bring back three of the vocalists who performed with the band. (L to r) Thora Anders, Lorraine and Juliette drew the cameras, and* Swing Is In, Vol II *was off to a rousing start.* Bill Cunningham photo

BCIT experience had given me more than a new profession. It had armed me with the weapons to take a different approach to the old one. I had management skills now that I could apply to the band. I knew how to approach potential sponsors and buyers, and knew that, even more so than in the past, the band business wasn't just about the music, it was about *selling* it, getting us into the public perception and keeping us there. I had two weapons as I launched the new Dal Richards: the sales and management techniques learned at BCIT, and that credo burned into my brain decades earlier by Ivan Ackery: "Don't forget the balcony!"

The gigs were starting to come in but, as desirable as they were and always had been and would be, I'd be working for someone else. And I had an idea: Why not work for myself? Run my own gigs, find co-sponsors, and place the band in venues where I knew it would work? Maybe the big bands weren't back as they'd been in the old days, but the great songs of that era were being sung by new artists and revived by the old. All those years on the bandstand had given me a solid instinct of what the audience wanted. Why not put that knowledge to work, do all the regular gigs, but pick my spots to stage my own?

By then I had my weekly radio show *Dal's Place* up and running on CHQM. Now, on the recommendation of sales director Brian Scharf, the station agreed to join me as co-sponsor of a series of tea dances in the Pacific Ballroom of the Hotel Vancouver. It was the beginning of what you might call the rebirth of the Dal Richards orchestra.

We played about ten New Year's Eve dances at (not for) the Bayshore Hotel, renting the facility and finding the sponsors. On the surface, nothing changed. The music was the same, the crowds danced in the New Year as they'd always done. But now we were in control. We weren't just into band music, we were in the band *business*—and have been ever since.

There was another major change: after all those years of thinking big band only, I realized that there was an untapped market out there for a small group—a quartet, say—that could appear in the smaller clubs, at birthdays, anniversaries, graduations, coming-out parties—events that didn't require a full band or the expense that would involve. I formed the Dal Richards Jazz Quartet: Ron Thompson on guitar, Jamie Croil on trumpet and vocals, Diane Lines on keyboard and vocals, and me on tenor sax and vocals plus a whole lot of commentary.

There's also a big market in seniors residences, where the thinking has changed on the type of entertainment brought in. We do a circuit once a year—my trapline, I call it: the Dogwood Pavilion in Coquitlam, Langley Gardens, Langley Senior Recreation Centre, the Newton Seniors Centre, the Peninsula Retirement Resort in White Rock (where one of the residents is John Townsend, who played trumpet in my band at the Roof in the '50s), Crofton Manor in Vancouver, the Fleetwood Villa in Surrey and the Gilmore Gardens in Richmond. The response is always tremendous. We hear some wonderfully heartfelt stories there from people who remember dancing at the Roof, in many cases with the loves of their lives. (There is, I must admit, another side to that coin: when the band does dances, one of the requests we get so often that it's become part of our band book is *The Second Time Around*, which Lorraine sang at the Roof, from people who have found true love more than once.) When the Coastal Jazz and Blues Society stages the Vancouver Jazz Festival it books the full band and singers plus guest Jim Byrnes for appearances on the Gastown stages and at David Lam Park. That's an accolade from one of the driving forces on the Vancouver music scene.

But, for all the new focus and business approach, we've never forgotten our musical roots, which, I believe, is one of the secrets of the band's longevity: we get involved in community activities—charities, openings, fundraisers and such. And, of course, anything that has to do with the encouragement and betterment of the local music scene. One of our favourites over the last few years occurs annually at the Chan Centre for the Performing Arts—a

*The Vancouver International Jazz Festival's reputation has grown to the point where it's recognized as one of the finest in the world—which makes our band more proud to be part of it each year.*

European-style masked ball dinner dance and fundraiser for the UBC Opera Society with one major difference added by UBC's professor of opera and voice, Nancy Hermiston. She asked me if I would bring my swing band.

It's worked out beautifully. Nancy's opera students perform, dinner is served, the band breaks into dance music and everyone sings, dances and has a wonderful time. And, for us, there's been a bonus: the discovery of operatic talents who also play, sing and love jazz. A tenor named Sonny Shams had been a jazz pianist and asked if he could do a number with us. He played and sang so well that I hired him to appear with us at the PNE. Simone Osborne, who won a competition at New York's Metropolitan Opera, also turned out to be a fine jazz vocalist.

In any business, part of the secret of success lies in building solid relationships. In June of 2004 we began one of the best with the Great Canadian Gaming Corp., and in particular with Howard Blank, vice-president of Media, Entertainment and Responsible Gaming. It started with a series of regular gigs in the Lulu Lounge of Richmond's River Rock Casino. Soon Howard also had us appearing at the Boulevard Casino in Coquitlam. Today we are the corporation's special events band and I am its official ambassador.

We play Mother's Day brunch and, of course, New Year's Eve, at River Rock, an amazing venue (designed by the people who created the Cirque du Soleil set) in which the seats are on hydraulics that can lower them flat into the floor to convert from theatre to dance floor in eight minutes;

and the acoustics make it a joy to play in. We also make appearances at the corporation's other venues, including the Cloverdale and Hastings Park race courses and the Boulevard Casino. To commemorate my ninetieth birthday my friends at Great Canadian ran a full-page ad in the *Vancouver Sun* and gave a generous donation to my foundation. This year I've been paid another honour: the Dal Richards suite will soon open in the River Rock showroom, fully catered and complete with concierge, decorated with Dal Richards memorabilia. People can rent the suite, watch the show and look at big band highlight photos collected over the years.

Let's take a minute here and introduce you to my current band. Rhythm section: Diane Lines, piano; Ron Thompson, guitar; Gary Mussatto, drums; Tim Stacey, bass. Sax: Jack Stafford, Saul Berson, Julia Nolan, Chris Startup, Bill Abbott and me (playing, as *Vancouver Sun* columnist and former sax player Mac Perry calls it every time he comes to one of our gigs, "the balanced-action Mark 7 Paris Selmer E-flat alto sax). Vocals: Diane, Bria, Jennifer Hayes, Jamie and me. Trumpet: Jamie Croil, Derry Byrne, Bria Skonberg, Ross Gregory. Trombone: Rob Fraser, Rob McKenzie, Rod Murray.

I can't say enough about this superbly talented group. I'm the meet-and-greet guy who sings a few songs, plays a couple of horns and tells a few stories—okay, maybe a lot of stories. They provide the solid, big-band sound that is my band. I count my blessings that I have them.

Has the transition from old Dal to new Dal been a success? The proof, as they say, is in the pudding: the band in its various forms is busier now and has more gigs per year than ever before. I truly believe that our new CD, *Dal Richards and Friends: One More Time!*, is the best thing we've ever done. And what was it Jimmy Durante used to say? "You ain't heard nothin' yet!"

But before we leave "Old Dal," let me tell you about my other job, and the wonderful tales it triggered, starting with this one…

It was one of those magical musical moments that rate a special niche in Vancouver's entertainment history: the wee hours of the morning on October 8, 1966, when Jack Wasserman, the *Vancouver Sun* saloon columnist (his term) strode to the microphone at centre stage of the Queen Elizabeth Theatre and sang *Embraceable You* in a voice so rich

*The first Variety Club telethon in 1966 drew a sellout crowd to the Queen Elizabeth Playhouse. As the telephone pledges rolled in we played on...and on...and on.... How many times can you play* When the Saints Go Marching In? *Jack Lindsay photo*

and splendid you wondered why he was wasting his time in the newspaper game when he could be out collecting recording royalties and fighting off groupies.

The occasion was the newly formed Vancouver chapter of Variety Club International's first fundraising telethon for its many children's charities. I was in the orchestra pit with my band, so I had one of the best seats in the house to watch Jack's performance unfold—close enough, in fact, to note with interest that Jack wasn't singing at all. He was lip-synching, and I knew why.

Jack's wife, Fran Gregory, could sing—show tunes, mostly, although she did do some pop vocals at local lounges and clubs. Jack couldn't, and had no interest in trying, but he was Variety's press guy for the telethon, and someone had just phoned in to pledge $150 if Jack would sing a duet with his wife. There was no way Jack was going to lose that money. Never mind that the televised show was on its way to raising a then-astonishing $66,000. Every penny counted.

Jack disappeared behind the curtain, reappeared in a few moments, and burst into song. But the voice wasn't his, it was that of Ed Ames, formerly of the Ames Brothers quartet and now carving himself a successful solo career when he wasn't otherwise occupied playing Mingo, Fess Parker's faithful Indian sidekick on the *Daniel Boone* TV series. Ed was one of the stars imported for the talent show, and he agreed to add *Embraceable You* to his repertoire from behind a curtain while Jack took the bows out front and the technical people made sure the sound came from the right place. And, yes, the $150 pledge was made good.

*With each passing year the Variety Club's* Show of Hearts *telethon has grown bigger and clearly a lot dressier than on that first hectic night. And each year, the donations for a great cause pour in.*

That telethon was in itself a miracle, given that Vancouver hadn't even *had* a Variety Club chapter until the spring of '65, when local theatre owner and manager Harry Howard strode into the Terminal City Club for his regular lunch with a bunch of old cronies and opened with "Okay, boys, I want twenty-five bucks from each of you." All nine men complied. Harry pocked the $225. "Congratulations," he said. "You are now charter members of the new Variety Club Children's Charities chapter."

But somehow the show was put together, thanks in large part to the big-name entertainers who were in town and jumped in to help. Patti Page, who was playing the Cave that week, didn't just appear—she brought her entire show, including Fraser MacPherson's band, and stayed until 4 a.m. singing her hits including, of course, *How Much is that*

*Doggie in the Window?* Maynard Ferguson came to the theatre after his show at Isy's and blew up a storm. Add the top local talent—Lance Harrison, Fraser MacPherson, Carse Sneddon and their bands, Eleanor Collins, Eve Smith, Lynne McNeil, Bill Kenny of the original Ink Spots, world yo-yo champion Harvey Lowe and so many others and you had a show that could stand on its own with any in the country. And, at a time when telethons were virtually unheard of locally, the money just rolled in.

My most vivid memory is the finale, when the producer came over about ten minutes from the scheduled closing time and told me to start playing *When the Saints Go Marching In* and keep it going until we went off the air because it kept

*Over the years the Variety Club telethon has drawn many stars from the entertainment world to perform and draw TV viewers and donors, including TV personality Mary Hart.* Jim Harrison photo

the phones ringing and the pledges coming in. He was right. The phones did keep ringing. But I have to admit that, as much as I like the tune, around about the twentieth repetition it was wearing a little thin on the band.

I joined Variety in the chapter's second year and have been happily active in it ever since, including a stretch from 1984 through 1987 when I was hired as its executive director. In those days, Barbara Stewart was chief barker (president). My buddy, Art Jones, was another. It was Art and his partners in Vantel Broadcasting who received the licence for Vancouver's first private television station, CHAN, channel 8.

I was with him when he got the news. He was thirty-four years old then, and he was still involved with television with his interview show, *Art Jones and Company* on Shaw cable, when he died at age eighty in 2006.

Each Christmas I climb into a Santa Claus suit and drop into Variety's special care ward at St. Paul's Hospital for premature-birth infants, where Dallas spent the first six weeks of her life, to sing Christmas songs and distribute gifts for the newborns and their mothers. (In 2008, one of the newborns Santa saw there was named Ella. "After Ella Fitzgerald," her mother, Tammy, explained. Further along was a baby named Harrison. "After Harrison Ford," said mom Nicola. Two show biz babies, cheek by jowl. Made me feel right at home.) There's also the Variety Christmas party for kids with disabilities. Young people there might have trouble walking or using their hands, but when the music starts—rock 'n' roll, swing, it doesn't matter—they come alive, hit the floor and no matter what their degree of

*My long-time buddy, Art Jones, was one of the quiet forces of the Vancouver media scene, a TV talk show host and the man who launched CHAN-TV. He and his wife Mary were also frequent companions in our madcap trips to Seattle.*

disability or limitation of movement the transformation is amazing. On the floor and in their hearts, they're *dancing*.

I've been fortunate enough to receive the local club's highest individual honour, the Golden Heart Award for community achievement, and a Pioneer Award for long and ongoing service in 2000. We've also played at affairs where others have been award recipients, including the one the night Jimmy Pattison received his Heart Award. The way it was supposed to work, the dinner party would be paraded in with Jimmy at the rear, but as the parade entered the room it became apparent that a key component was missing. Jimmy was nowhere to be seen. You could hear the murmurs in the crowd: "Where's Pattison?" "Where's Jimmy?" At that point, Jimmy stood up in my brass section where we'd hidden him and began blowing a solo on—what else?—*When the Saints Go Marching In*.

When the tireless Grace McCarthy, the first woman member of Variety International, received her Golden Heart, one song came to mind. Grace had been the driving force behind getting the lights strung on the Lions Gate Bridge—dubbed "Grace's Pearls" by the media. So, naturally, we played Glenn Miller's *A String of Pearls*.

We also play regularly at the fundraising dinner held by the Doormen of Greater Vancouver, where an honorary doorman is named and all proceeds go to C.H.I.L.D (Children with Intestinal and Liver Disorders) Foundation, of which Grace is a co-founder. There's also an auction, at which my wife Muriel bid $2,500 for a motor scooter—and won it. She gave it to he daughter Kayce, and the money went to a great cause.

In 2005 I was named the honorary doorman. Grace added a marvellous surprise, presenting me with the Roof Lounge sign that had hung on the wall during my years at the Panorama Roof. It was removed when the Roof closed, but Grace talked the hotel management into turning it over to her for the presentation. The sign, which must weigh at least forty pounds, now hangs on our wall at home. The attached plaque reads: *"Presented to Dal Richards from his many friends in the Variety Club.* Every time I look at it, it brings back another memory.

Variety membership has added special moments to my life over the years, moments too numerous to count. I'd bet that people in other service clubs would tell you the same thing about the good feelings they get from pitching in where there's a need and coming out with a sense of having helped.

*The first thing guests saw getting off the elevator at the Panorama Roof was the sign for the lounge. It was presented to me in 1998, at my eightieth birthday party, a fundraiser for Variety, the Children's Charity, held at the Roof.*

One such organization close to our hearts is PAL, the Performing Arts Lodge, that provides subsidized housing for seniors whose careers have been in the entertainment industry. Spearheaded by actor/director Joy Coghill, the lodge is part of the Bayshore Gardens in Coal Harbour and contains twelve front-facing two-bedroom suites that were sold to help subsidize the rest of the project. The purchases come with strict conditions: only people who've been in the performing arts can apply. There are no mortgages, and no profit can be made. Muriel and I bought one together where, according to our plan, she will live out her years after I'm gone. Should we ever decide to sell, we can take only the amount we put in. Any additional money from the sale goes into the PAL subsidy fund.

It's a wonderful project full of spirited residents with the type of zaniness you might expect from show people staying active. Among those in residence are Joy, Roma Hearn, Lorraine Foster, Don Stewart, Judy Walchuk, June Katz, Patricia Duval, Ellie O'Day and Dave and Diane Forsythe-Abbott.

*It's become a Christmas highlight for me, my annual role as Santa Claus for a visit to the special care ward for prematurely born infants at St. Paul's Hospital. You just never know where you'll find an adorable little one.*
Stuart Davis photo, *Vancouver Sun*

# CHAPTER 11

# The Hit-Makers

*"Tell you about Dal? Well, the first words that come to me: he's not human. Something's not right in there. He's ninety-one, and at thirty-three my posture isn't as good as his.*

*It's amazing to see what he's done and the span over which he's done it. My grandfather had always hoped that some day I'd get to meet Dal—my grandfather! Then I entered the PNE Youth Talent Search and there he was, larger than life. I was very nervous and Dal is one cool customer. He was always kind and very classy. I mean, I was seventeen or eighteen and he was DAL RICHARDS. It was a good six or seven years before I realized whether he liked me or not because he was so kind of mellow. Never rude or anything like it, but his concentration level on a gig was almost robotic. It wasn't until I got to his apartment a couple of times that I got to meet the real Dal—warm, engaging, funny. On the job I never got any of that. I never thought he was a BAD man or anything like that, I just never knew WHAT he was.*

*I did quite a few gigs with Dal. It was such a neat feeling to be this young kid and get up there with this great big band and get to sing for those big audiences—mixed, not just older people, a lot of kids, which proved to me that this music I was singing was palatable to everyone. And now here's Dal at ninety-one, it's the same music, he's playing the same stuff he always did, and they still love it! He's helped to keep it alive. How many other kinds of music will be out there that long?*

*There are a lot of us out here (whom he's influenced) including David Foster. We're proud of him, and honoured to have been there. Let's hope there's another decade, another thousand gigs and more. It's such an incredible story, and I love the fact that I was able to be a small part of it. Give him our love."*

Michael Bublé

If the talent shows flooding the TV screens over the last few years prove one thing, it is that the planet is loaded with great musical talent, much of which never gets the chance to prove its quality. No matter what the old farmer's adage says, the cream *doesn't* always rise to the top. Sometimes it just hangs there in the middle of the bottle and no amount of shaking gets it to the top where it can be savoured and enjoyed.

Sometimes, though, if you're really lucky, you get a chance to shake the bottle and make a difference...

About a dozen years ago I was at the Victoria Jazz Festival, which ended with a pianorama, a kind of musical shoot-out in which pianists from the various bands in the festival are each given fifteen minutes to perform as soloists in their own style. As master of ceremonies, I'm looking down the list of entrants and their backgrounds so I'll have something to use for introductions. At the bottom there's a single line, just a name: Michael Kaeshammer. Not a word about who he is, where he's from, or what his background is. Just the name.

I went looking for him. He was nineteen, he said, born in Germany, studied classical piano until he was thirteen. Then his dad brought home a J.P. Johnson boogie-woogie record. "From that moment on," he said, "I was in love."

He'd provided no background information because, well, he'd heard about the showcase at the last minute and he'd just been playing in some of the local pubs anyway, jobs he'd begun to get after a long stretch of going from club to club and asking the managers to listen to tapes he'd made in his parents' basement.

Michael was the last to perform. He sat down and played a boogie version of *Tico Tico*. When he finished there was about five seconds of total silence. Then the place exploded. The audience went crazy. Bonnie Morgan, the pianist with the Wooden Nickel band, had tears in her eyes. "Nobody should be that good," she whispered.

Michael Kaeshammer is a big deal now, with CDs and hit gigs, but he has never forgotten that day or what it led to. Two stories:

In 2008 he came in from Toronto, where he is now based, to be a guest performer at the party celebrating the twentieth anniversary of Rick Hansen's epic wheelchair journey around the world. Jim Taylor, who'd written Hansen's book, heard Michael for the first time, introduced himself, and mentioned that he knew Muriel and me.

*When I first heard Michael Kaeshammer about a dozen years ago in Victoria he was just another kid playing the local clubs. Now he's a hugely popular jazz pianist and singer, a rising star who's never forgotten the folks he met along the way.*

"Are they here?" Michael asked. "I've got to see them!"

Muriel had been the public relations person for the Hansen tour. Taylor found her and brought her over. After hugs, Muriel told him of the plans for my ninetieth birthday gig.

"I'll be there," he said.

Muriel explained that there were as yet no details or location, and what with Michael's hectic schedule the committee was going to wait till there was something definite and...

"Doesn't matter," he said. "I'll be there." And he was.

Flash forward to May 5, 2008. Michael is opening for Anne Murray at the Queen Elizabeth Theatre. We're backstage talking and I mention that I'll be taking part in

BC's 150th birthday celebration on August 4, doing an open air show on the front lawn of the legislative buildings featuring people like Burton Cummings, Colin James, Sarah McLaughlin, Leslie Feist...

"I'm going to be in Victoria that day on my way to Beijing for the Olympics," he says.

Well, now. "Can you appear on the show?" I asked.

"Well, that's a problem, Dal," he said. "Those things have to be booked in advance now. My manager would kill me."

Time for Plan B.

"If you happened to be in the crowd, and I happened to notice you and I said, 'There's Michael Kaeshammer, folks. How about coming up and playing something, Michael?'..."

He grinned.

"Well, if that happened..."

Came August 4. We'd had trouble contacting Michael to confirm his appearance. No phone messages, no e-mails, nothing. I'd promised him I wouldn't tell a soul until I saw him there. The show was to start at noon, and at 11:57 there he was in the front row of the crowd. We shouldn't have worried. He'd said he'd be there.

I pretended to spot him, looked surprised, and went into the routine. Michael came onstage, played not one number, but two—Count Basie's *Red Bank Boogie* and *Tico Tico*—and brought the house down as he always does. He is a special talent, and a special young man.

A lot of people around today will tell you they knew right away that Michael Bublé was going to make it big in the music business. Well, anyone who heard him could see that. Everyone in my band who played behind him would nod and say this kid was going to get there. But when we said it we were thinking Las Vegas, that the kid was good enough to play the casinos some day soon. But *no one* could have anticipated CD and DVD sales in the millions worldwide, the stardom, the sold-out concerts, the TV appearances. He was just this sixteen-year-old who entered the PNE Youth Talent Search, sang Sinatra standards he'd heard on his granddad's old records and liked so much that he sang them karaoke style to musical back tracks.

Hugh Pickett and I alternated on a panel of judges for the show, which I saw only sometimes because we were playing tea dances in the Garden Auditorium in the afternoons when it was on. Hugh was judging when Michael sang. "There's a kid you should hear," he said later. "Sings like Sinatra." Then Beverly Delich, who was shepherding Michael in those days, told me about him. "How about using him at the PNE tea dances in the Garden building?" she asked. Well, why not?

That was Michael's first appearance, at one of our tea dances. I was the first to pay him for a gig, but I don't recall how much. He appeared with us for a couple of years, and again when we moved outdoors onto the big stage. When he came back from a two-year stint in California I hired him again, this time at $250 per gig.

In 1999 I got an idea: How about staging a show called Stars of the New Millennium starring the two Michaels,

*Michael Bublé's career really began when he won the PNE's talent search show as a sixteen-year-old crooning Frank Sinatra tunes. Today he's a superstar. And to think I gave him his first paying gig.* Dave Roels photo

Bublé on vocals, Kaeshammer on piano? I approached the Vancouver Symphony with the idea of staging it at the Orpheum, produced it, and it was so well received that Pickett presented me with his ticket to frame and hang on my wall, a special remember-when. He also mentioned— and remember, now, this was Hugh Pickett, who'd seen *everything*—that he hadn't heard such a buzz in the lobby at intermission in years.

Now, of course, Michael K is a star on the rise and Michael B is a mega-star, a young man who somehow found a niche that CD and DVD buyers and show patrons needed filled. There have been Sinatra sound-alikes before—men like Harry Connick Jr., whose work on the sound track of *When Harry Met Sally* opened the door to instant stardom, sit-com and movie roles, and made him one of those "overnight success" stories, never mind that he'd been a jazz piano phenom in New Orleans since childhood, when he once shared a piano and a duet with the legendary Eubie Blake. But none ever hit with the impact of this kid from Vancouver who loved to sing the old songs and dared to dream that it could be a full-time job. It's nice to know I played a part in launching both careers.

There are times, of course, when Canadian-born talents choose to stay in Canada when their abilities clearly prove that they belong with the best anywhere. Such was the case with Eleanor Collins, whose distinguished vocal career won her the sobriquet "the Canadian Lena Horne."

Eleanor grew up in Alberta singing around the piano. "I was going to music school," she says. "I just never realized it." In 1939, at age twenty, she moved to Vancouver, sang with various vocal groups, and made her TV debut on the CBC in 1954 on a variety show called *Eleanor*. A year later she became the first black woman and jazz singer to host her own weekly musical show, *The Eleanor Show*—one year before Nat King Cole, to much fuss and controversy, became the first black entertainer to host a weekly show on a US network. Today she can look back on a groundbreaking career that included headlining the 1975 Dominion Day celebrations on Parliament Hill, and singing *Look to the Rainbow* with the Tommy Banks orchestra on the CBC in 1980.

The little girl who sang around the family piano has been recognized by the city of Vancouver with a Distinguished Pioneer award.

Eleanor's sister, Pearl Brown, an aunt of legendary blues guitarist Jimi Hendrix, made her own mark as a blues singer in Vancouver. Pearl had appeared with Theatre Under the Stars in plays like *Raisin in the Sun*, but didn't begin singing professionally until she was sixty-one. Her son, Henri, who has made his own musical mark with his band, HB Concept, which is huge in Asia, produced her first record in 1962: *Black Cultured Pearl*. It sold only 2,000 copies or so, but drew the attention of Wynton Marsalis, who was performing at Expo and had her sing with his band whenever he came to Vancouver and made a record with her, *Wynton and Pearl: Goin' Down Home*.

Black performers coming to Vancouver knew Pearl for another reason, as they knew Edwina Jones, whose own daughter, Sugar, became a vocalist who did extensive backup work with some of the big names of the Motown era: Edwina and Pearl cooked soul food to die for, not exactly readily available in the downtown hotels and clubs. Through the '40s, people like Count Basie, Duke Ellington, the Mills Brothers, Sarah Vaughan, Sammy Davis Jr. and, later, Diana Ross during an appearance at the Cave were regulars at the big house on Joyce Road. They'd bring the ingredients, Pearl or Edwina would prepare it. Often, the guests bunked there overnight.

There have been all sorts of music-related success stories in this province over the years, but maybe the biggest of all concerns a man who hasn't got a lot of time to play his horn these days but has never lost his love of the music and its history.

Without question, Jimmy Pattison is one of the city's icons. Self-made billionaire, sure. The man in charge of Expo 86, right. The guy who went looking for a bigger house in Palm Springs and wound up buying the Frank Sinatra compound lock, stock and barrel. Okay. But to me he's another musician who came out of Arthur Delamont's Kits band some years after I did, and hasn't grown too big to haul out his trumpet and blow for fun, for charity, or to help to say "Happy Birthday" to a ninety-year-old saxophone player and throw in his own special grand finale.

Peter Legge tells that one best.

> At the dinner dance in the BC Ballroom the night of Dal's actual ninetieth birthday there'd been some individual $1,000 donations to the Dal Richards Foundation. Now I'm backstage at the Orpheum birthday concert the next day with Jimmy and Michael Kaeshammer and a bunch of other performers and organizers and Jimmy asks how much money was raised. It was $83,000, and Dal pledged $17,000 to make it the even $100,000.
>
> "Were you in for $1,000?" he asks.
>
> Yes, I tell him, I was in for $1,000. Then, just as he's about to go onstage to blow Happy Birthday I say, "Jimmy, you're a hundred times wealthier than me." Maybe a thousand times might have been more accurate.
>
> We have no idea what he's got planned other than Happy Birthday. But he plays, it, and at the finish draws an envelope from his breast pocket, then announces that he's donating $100,000 to the Foundation. One hundred thousand dollars! But that's Jimmy...

*Jimmy Pattison takes time away from his duties as CEO of Expo '86 to pick up his pocket trumpet to play* When the Saints Go Marching In.

Ah, those horn players. Jimmy walked out on stage, played and led the audience in *Happy Birthday*, then made the announcement of the $100,000. Muriel and Dallas were with me onstage. It left us speechless.

Jimmy's love affair with music began as a kid when he started playing the horn in a skid row church where his dad worked at night for many years with down-and-outers because he'd been one himself until his life got turned around through the church. Jimmy played there, and through high school and at UBC. There was a year in there at fifteen when he had his appendix out and couldn't blow the horn but, being Jimmy, he saw an ad in the paper offering twenty lessons for $40, signed up and learned to play piano to keep the music going until he was strong enough to pick up the trumpet.

His life story has been well documented, from the decade and more on the street selling cars, through the purchase of his first dealership, radio station CJOR and on to become one of the country's richest men and an international business powerhouse. But I think first of the musician who used to listen to our radio broadcasts from the Panorama Roof, the man I first met at a Kitsilano band reunion, the man who had the chance to buy the place Sinatra bought in 1957, where the Rat Pack and so many others hung out, and made the decision in forty-five minutes plus flight time from Palm Springs to Penticton.

A real estate lady had asked him if he was interested in a bigger residence. They looked at one that didn't turn him on. Well, she said, she had another one, but he'd have to sign a confidentiality agreement on where he'd been and what he'd seen. He had time to look it over before he rushed to the airport to make his flight. By the time the plane landed he'd made up his mind, phoned, and made an offer.

Muriel and I have been his guests there, and it's magnificent. The memorabilia alone takes your breath away. But for Jimmy it's also a great place to hold business meetings. People who could afford to stay anywhere are absolutely overwhelmed. Sinatra's digs *and* a shrewd business deal. How great is that?

I was on my way for a coffee last spring in the Griffins restaurant in the Hotel Vancouver, which adjoins the Hornby Street entrance, when two burly obvious security

*Given a chance to visit the compound once owned by Frank Sinatra that was the frequent hangout for the Rat Pack and other entertainment legends, who could resist sitting in Frank's director's chair? Not me.*

types stopped me. "Just wait here a minute, sir," one of them said.

"I'm just going to the restaurant," I said.

"Just wait here, sir," he repeated. "It will only be a few minutes."

"Some sort of celebrity coming?" I asked innocently.

"Just wait here," he said.

Just then, a woman enters, baby in arms. It's Diana Krall, the Nanaimo pianist/singer who's become an international star. Behind her is her husband, Elvis Costello. Well, I've known Diana for a long time. I wave and yell, "Diana! It's Dal!"

The security men are not impressed. But Diana pivots, breaks ranks. "Well, hello!" she says, and we exchange hugs.

It can't be easy, staying regular folks when you've become a household word and the spotlight is seldom off you. Some never manage, others never forget their roots. The degree of fame isn't the criterion. It's said that Frank Sinatra's advance list of requirements for an appearance was only slightly shorter than *The Rise and Fall of the Roman Empire*. On the other hand, publicist Jack Lee, with whom I also worked at the PNE, remembers that when Ella Fitzgerald played the Cave all she wanted was lemon slices and ice water. When Lee was sent to the airport to greet and assist the Beatles for their 1964 PNE appearance he found four young men who couldn't have been easier to work with. But you also get people on the lower rungs of the entertainment ladder who act as though they're at the very top.

That's why Diana's hug was special. Clearly, the girl from Nanaimo hadn't been swept away.

Rick Hansen was once asked to explain the difference between *handicap* and *disability*. "My disability is that I cannot use my legs," he said. "My handicap is your perception of that, and thus of me." My friend Jim Byrnes would understand that. He lost both his legs at age twenty-three when hit from behind by a car while helping to push a stalled truck off the highway. It slowed him, but it didn't stop him as he built and continues a long successful career as singer, blues guitarist and television actor.

Jim was born and raised in St. Louis, and the music was always with him, first piano, then the guitar that helped him find his way back from the devastation of his physical condition. "The guitar let me forget for a while," he says. "It made the pain go away." One of his fondest memories of those days was going to a club as a kid to hear Muddy Waters and having the man himself sit down, talk to him and buy him a Coke. Jim performs all over the world. His list of bookings is staggering. But whenever I phone and ask him to appear with us, his answer is four words long: "I will be there."

Remembrance Day performance at the Orpheum? "I'll be there."

Find time to guest with us at the PNE? "I'll be there."

Be a part of our new CD? "I'll be there."

*St. Louis Blues?* "Sounds good."

One day I just had to ask. "You've got so much work. You're always up to your neck in bookings. But when I ask, you always say yes. I'm delighted and grateful—but how come?"

He just looked at me.

"Man!" he said, "do I *love* singing with your big band!"

We'd both appeared on one of the Kerrisdale Days shows, and met again in 1983 when Jim, Juliette and I were the judges at one of the PNE's talent shows: the usual thing—singers, dancers, etc., all under the avid gaze of parents who thought their child was the clear winner. But in that day's group there was a magician so good that, as Jim said, "This guy could go to Vegas and get work!" So we named him the winner, and wondered for a second if we were going to get out of the place alive.

Since then, Jim's always found time to be there for us. The latest example came last May when he came home

*Bluesman Jim Byrnes is never too busy to play and sing with my band, and the band likes backing him up as much as he loves singing with them. Here he cuts loose with* St. Louis Blues *at my ninetieth birthday bash.*

from an exhausting Asian tour and within a week was joining us in the recording of *Dal Richards and Friends, One More Time! w*here he sang a Bill Runge arrangement of *St. Louis Blues,* which is a gut-buster for our trumpet section of Derry Byrne, Jamie Croil and Bria Skonberg. But they dig doing it for Jim. It's a reciprocal admiration society: he loves to sing with the band, and the band loves to perform with him. We both consider ourselves fortunate.

# Them's the Breaks

*"If a band doesn't get work, it doesn't exist. Dal has always taken it as a personal challenge to find work for his band, and geared his music to what his audience is looking for, which is something he just* knows. *We weren't always a show band, but one night in the mid-'80s I asked him if I could sing* Kansas City. *He said yes. That started people coming out of the band to sing or standing up to solo. We became what we are today because Dal saw that the people liked it and understood that it could work. Call it instinct, call it whatever you like. It works, and that's Dal."*

Jamie Croil, trumpet, arranger and vocals.

These days you see them everywhere: guys playing instruments—sometimes well, more often not—a case or a hat or a paper cup on the sidewalk in front of them in a silent plea for pocket change. The violinist sawing away, head down, in front of the Broadway liquor store was no different. But as I dropped a bill into his case, without looking up or missing a beat, he said "Thanks, Dal." And I thought, "There, but for the grace of God...."

Getting a spot in a band or in front of a microphone is a crapshoot. There are always more horn players, pianists and vocalists than there are spots to put them. As the current glut of TV talent shows proves, there are hundreds, maybe thousands, of superbly gifted musicians and singers out there who, for whatever reason, never get an opportunity to show it. You also have to be lucky—and sometimes that luck works both ways.

About ten years ago I was walking down 41st Avenue in Kerrisdale, heading for a stage set up on Yew Street to celebrate Kerrisdale Days, an annual show where they block off the street and people swarm the area to take in the entertainment. I passed a little Dixieland trio playing on the street corner. The trombone caught my ear. This guy was *good*. When the number ended I asked him if he'd like to sit in with my band. His name was Rod Murray. He's been with the band ever since and plays with major jazz groups all over the country.

I found Jennifer Hayes the same way, heading into Tourism Vancouver's annual open house with Rick Antonson. This girl was singing with a small group in the lobby. I got about twenty feet past them before her voice registered. I stopped dead.

"Who is *that?*" I asked him.

"She works here at the bureau, and is on our international sales team for the eastern US in Washington DC," Rick said, and took me back for an introduction. "With a job like that, I wonder if she'd be interested in singing with the band?" I thought. But it cost nothing to try. About a week later I saw Rick again at the annual Wake-Up Award breakfast held by the Vancouver AM Tourism Association held to honour someone who has fostered tourism in the city. I was the recipient in 2007. "Guess who I just had coffee with?" I said. "Jennifer Hayes. She's gonna sing with the band."

Jennifer was an instantaneous hit. I particularly remember a breakfast roast for Vancouver mayor Philip Owen. It's 7 a.m. and out sways Jennifer in a slinky gown singing Peggy Lee's *Fever*. She is an attractive young lady. You could almost see the steam forming on the mayor's glasses.

We are a stage show band as opposed to a dance band. That means individual performers step up for more than instrumental solos. Versatility counts. When Bria Skonberg puts down her trumpet, Diane Lines leaves the piano and they join Jennifer in front of a microphone centre stage to sing *Jump, Jive and Wail* so well that Louis Jordan, who had the hit with his Tympany Five, would have given them a standing ovation. It's the talent that shines through first, but the fact that they're gorgeous is a glorious bonus. That's not sexism, it's show biz.

Diane's trip to that stage took a little longer. I'll let her tell it:

> I'd heard about Dal almost all my life. My mom used to sneak out of the nurses' residence during the Second World War so the officers would take them to the Roof for an evening of dancing and a good steak dinner.

*She was with me the first time I met him. I was sitting at the piano during a Christmas concert at a mall. He introduced himself and handed me his card—I still remember that red card—chatted a bit and said to give him a call. My mom ran up and said 'Migawd, that was Dal Richards!' She was so excited. But I never called him. I was too scared. What would I say?*

*Four years or so later I was playing a gig at the Cloud Nine at the Sheraton Landmark. He came over again, we chatted, and he wound up booking us in the Pan Pacific as a duo. From then on he'd hire me for the odd thing when he needed a pianist.*

*Then, on the Remembrance Day just before his eighty-fifth birthday, I was playing for Gillian Campbell. Dal and I were chatting again. "So," I asked, "when are you going to hire me for the big band?"*

*"I do have a gig that might work," he said. It was me on piano, Dal on sax and singing. We just clicked. And, after a few more gigs, he trusted me enough to put me in the band when an opening came up. We do big band, trios, duets—and it's been a joyful journey.*

Diane has one detail wrong: she didn't wait for an opportunity. I created one. Talent like that, you don't wait, you grab.

I mentioned show biz, and that special sense of pizzazz. The girls have it. So did Kai Basanta. Once again, I grabbed.

About four years ago Jamie Croil, our trumpeter/vocalist, hung around for the talent show that follows our performance at the PNE. "Heard someone you might be interested in," he told me the next day. "He's a drummer in a little rock group. Might be worth talking to." He was. After hearing him perform with the group I introduced myself. "Want to sit in with my band and do a battle of the drummers with Gary Mussatto on *Sing, Sing, Sing?*" I asked.

"Sure," he said, nonchalantly. Hey, what's to be scared of when you're fourteen years old? We cleared it with his parents, he did the gig, held his own with Gary, and he's been with us off and on ever since, including at my ninetieth birthday show.

Kai was the first winner of a $2,000 scholarship from the Coastal Jazz and Blues Society, which I fund, for those planning to further their careers by attending a musical college. Remember the name, because he is going places. When Killarney Senior Secondary School decided this year not to send its band to Toronto for the annual MusicFest Canada festival for high school bands in Canada, Kai sent an audition tape to organizers, who were so impressed they flew him out to play with the Yamaha all-star band in the festival's grand finale. In that all-star band with him was this year's scholarship winner, sax and clarinet player Brian Rapanos of Handsworth Senior Secondary School in North Vancouver. Second of our three scholarship winners to date was trumpeter Eli Bennett. When he played with our band at David Lam Park, our guys couldn't believe that a sixteen-year-old could be that advanced.

It isn't just the performers who have to be lucky. What about the band leaders?

I was invited to attend an awards ceremony at the Centre for the Performing Arts where students at Capilano College were to receive their scholarships. The top award went to a trumpet player named Bria Skonberg, a beautiful blonde young lady I couldn't help but notice. Then I learned that her scholarship was not just for playing the trumpet, but also for vocals, arranging and music theory, for all of which she was presented with the 2006 CBC Jazz Award of Merit. My radar went *ping!* Maybe I should be talking to her. Her parents Owen and Chris were there. I went over and introduced myself to her family. We talked for a while and Bria spoke of playing in the Capilano "A" band. If she could hold a seat in that group I knew she could fit in anywhere. So I mentioned that my band would be playing a Mother's Day gig at the River Rock Casino, which was a week away. Would she like to sit in?

"Sure," she said.

There was no rehearsal. I just dropped her into our powerhouse brass section and she nailed it. What a performer.

To hear Bria tell it, she was living on a hobby farm in Chilliwack, got this horn, scared all the horses and chickens in the neighbourhood and had to move to Vancouver where she got into the music program at Cap and, presto! Not quite. A staggering amount of work goes into those college sessions, and Bria came out of them with a degree in jazz performance. She's gone on to work in youth jazz camps, given lectures at, among other places, Sacramento State U and U of Colorado, and plays all over the world. In 2007 she won the Kobe Jazz Friendship Award, presented at the Breda Jazz Festival in Holland. If she deafened any farm animals, they gave their ears to a great cause.

Maybe it's because I remember the jump start I got performing with Mr. D and the Kits band and the benefits of daring to push the envelope along the way, but I get a big kick out of watching the young people come along, some cocky, some scared, but all burning with the desire to perform.

These days, Paul Airey is a composer-producer and owner of The Sound Kitchen, home studio for *Dal's Place* and the kettle in which so much electronic magic is brewed. I remember him as a fifteen-year-old who showed up at the Hotel Georgia where I was director of sales, asked to speak to me, and said he'd written a song for the Variety Club telethon. He'd taken classical piano, he explained, "but not well enough, so I started composing." His brother and bass player, Howard, was with him with an amp and his bass, which they'd carted on the bus and, unlike me with my sax, managed to take with them when they got off.

"You go into the main ballroom and wait," my secretary told them. I came in a few minutes later. They played and sang it for me, a pretty good song, and were, to quote Paul, "terrible."

"Don't go anywhere," I said, and came back in fifteen minutes with two other players who joined in as they played it again. Two weeks later the telethon people called Paul and told him I wanted to play his song on the show and had a singer, Loretta Marlene, who would love to sing it. We did the full rehearsal at the Queen Elizabeth Theatre with the boys sitting on the apron of the stage at the edge of the orchestra pit. Five minutes before the show I turned to my pianist, Bud Henderson, and said, "Let the kid play."

This fifteen-year-old climbed in there with his idols, people like Oliver Gannon, Lance Harrison and Fraser MacPherson. They played his song and he played right along with them. Playing or watching, you can't buy moments like that.

That's how you build a band. You create a nucleus (and mine is top drawer) and add the special pieces as they come along. Some stay, some move on. David Foster played bass in my band briefly before going off to Los Angeles to launch that incredible career as songwriter and producer/arranger for people like Barbra Streisand. Michael Bublé won the PNE talent show, I spoke to Beverly Delich, and he was singing with us the next day and many times thereafter.

Maybe I've developed an instinct for discovering young talent. More likely I'm still blessed with the mystical powers of all those horseshoes from my father's blacksmith shop. No matter. The talent has arrived and I've been privileged to help it along and to watch it develop. That may be the most important gig of all. If ever I were to forget that, I have a thin, hand-written partial memoir to remind me.

In the Delamont family, the genes ran true. Mr. D was a builder who constructed and led the Kitsilano Boys Band. His son, Gordon, was a musical genius, particularly as a music arranger, who took his trumpet to Toronto and passed that genius on. Ask any of Toronto's major players of the day. They will tell you how much they owe Gordon and his teachings.

*Beverly Delich, who was guiding Michael Bublé in the early days, suggested that I hire him to sing with the band at the Garden Auditorium. Who knew that within a decade he would be selling millions of CDs and be mobbed by fans around the world?*

Gordon died much too young of a heart attack in 1981. His legacy, in addition to the talents he helped develop in so many of this country's finest musicians, includes two textbooks, *Modern Harmonic Technique Volumes 1 & 2*, examining the contemporary techniques of tonal harmony for arrangers and composers, and an unfinished memoir, sadly only seven chapters long, sent to me by Gordon's widow, Vida after his death.

Naturally, I looked to see whether I was in it. Gordon's first professional job was as a trumpet player with my band at the Palomar Ballroom. Maybe there'd be something in the manuscript that would provide insight on the view from orchestra to band leader rather than the other way around. Sure enough:

*I became a professional musician, a matter of joining a musicians' union, in the mid-'30s, and after playing with a few Vancouver orchestras became involved with Dal Richards and his orchestra. Dal had a major role in shaping my attitudes in the music business. He provided me with the opportunity to learn the basics of lead trumpet player and the basics of the crafts of composing and arranging. I was able to write music for his orchestra and hear it played by professional musicians in professional circumstances. Furthermore, he was the first person to pay me for writing music.*

*As valuable as all this was, it was the attitude to the music business that I gained from Dal that was even more important…he imbued in me a feeling for the glamour of the music business and the pure joy of being a musician. He never actually talked of these things but it was implicit in his demeanour, his bearing and his leadership. Although Dal was never what could be called an A-1 musician, he played the saxophone and clarinet with competence and was a much better than average popular singer in the style of the day. Mostly, though, he was a good leader with an ability to keep the management, the musicians and the public we were playing for all reasonably happy. This ability is just as rare now as it was then…*

*Dal Richards is, I am happy to say, still involved in music in Vancouver as well as being in the business of hotel management, knowledge about which he acquired from formal study and also from being orchestra leader at the Panorama Roof in the Hotel Vancouver for twenty-five consecutive years (which is certainly a record in this country and, quite possibly, in the world!). In any case most musicians usually have a Dal Richards figure somewhere near the beginning of their careers. I am happy that my personal Dal Richards was the genuine article.*

A fair assessment. I'm a good musician, not a great one—but I've recognized potential and *hired* great ones or those who one day would be. I'm not an arranger, so I've hired arrangers who were or would be great. My real strength, I think, has been in outlining for those arrangers how I want the band to sound.

Jamie Croil has been a band member for twenty years. For the past seven years he's also been our prime music arranger. When you hear the band you are hearing the shape and sound Jamie has produced. When I want to include a new song I confer with the singer, then with Jamie as to how I want it to sound, and he produces the sound and the feel I've asked for.

Part of my job and our success lies in the managing and promotion that keep us working. And, of course, the conscious decision to stay in Vancouver rather than head east or south as others did. People became familiar with us. We're a thread in the local fabric to the point where, in the last couple of decades, we've become, well, an institution.

But isn't it funny how things come full circle. Mr. D imbued me with that same joy and sense of glamour of the music business, and a generation later I was able to pass those feelings along to his son. Karma? Who knows? But reading those handwritten words puts a good feeling in my heart.

An awful lot has been written over the years about the great bands, the great tunes and the great musicians who play them. Not much that I've read mentions the work. It's understandable, for the people who attend our PNE shows or any of the dance or concert gigs we play are there for the product, not the process. But anyone who's been involved in assembling a band will tell you a great truth: First, you put the band together. Then the real work starts.

Remember me telling you about the time in '39 when I was with the Stan Patton band in Edmonton, the Tivoli theatre burned down and we lost our music library? That wasn't an inconvenience. That was a disaster. A band's library—or "book" to give it its proper name—is as vital as its instruments. My band's book today contains the music for about two hundred songs, of which we'll use perhaps thirty or forty a show. Because I'm usually pretty sure of the musical taste of the audience at a given show, the favourites are near the front. But you've always got to be ready for the requests, the calls for numbers that *aren't* in the book that someone out there remembers singing or hearing back in the day.

We have an edge. Both guitar player Ron Thompson and Diane Lines spent a lot of time playing the cruise ships, where taking requests is a key component of an entertainer's performance. I've yet to hear them stumped by a request for which they haven't the basic melody so the rest of the rhythm section can jump in and carry on. It's not a skill you pick up quickly. It's the result of an accumulation of knowledge won the hard way, by playing every type of song in every type of situation. And if there *is* a song with which they're not familiar, you can bet Jennifer or Bria or Jamie will be.

But in the midst of all that, you've got to be prepared to change, to meet the demands of a market that might be shifting, as it often has over the decades we've been around. Again, you have to have the personnel. Jamie's vocals—and his dazzling scat renditions—have become a big part of our transition into a show band in which band members solo, combine for trios and duets and are always willing to try new things. Gary Mussatto and young Kai Basanta do their battle of the drums on *Sing, Sing, Sing.* Diane is a great singer as well as a keyboard player. Jennifer can sing the lights out. Bria would be in this band on trumpet even if she

*Dal Richards and his Orchestra, including (l to r) Diane Lines, Jennifer Hayes and Bria Skonberg, cutting loose during BC's sesquicentennial celebration, with a concert on the lawn of the Parliament buildings.* Adrian Armstrong photo

couldn't sing, but when Diane leaves the keyboard, Bria puts down the trumpet, and they step to the mic with Jennifer and become a hot vocal trio, it's dynamite, and I think that's part of what's made us what we are—a show band.

No band in the country has a seventeen-day, two-shows-a-day gig. Not ever. But we have one every year at the PNE. We went from being one of the bands doing the tea dances in the Garden Auditorium to becoming the feature at the outdoor theatre at least partially because we were willing to change and the other bands weren't, or didn't. Patrick Roberge, the creative director for all aspects of the PNE's yearly concert and entertainment packages, recognizes what we bring to the table and keeps asking us back, which is a tribute in itself because no one has a better nose for what's hot and what the people want than Patrick, who chooses all the acts for the stage shows that draw nightly packed houses, and performs the same duties for Disneyland and Disney World. We open as the gates do and play for an hour for people who watch and listen on their way to the rest of the fair. They come back for the second show, which starts right after the pig races. I ask you, how many bands can claim they open for the pig races?

When you stay in one job for as long as we have with the PNE it becomes more than a job. Friendships are made. There's a sense of family. So, naturally, when Patrick Roberge's assistant, Anna Lam—Director of Corporate Development is her official title "but we don't go in for titles much around here"—announced her engagement, I volunteered the band to play at her wedding reception at the Vancouver Rowing Club. Anna and husband Simon Bond wanted a simple ceremony and had one request: "Play the same music you play at the PNE, and make it sound just like it does on the stage." Which, of course, we were happy to do. It was one swinging wedding.

Mike Daniel, the PNE's president and CEO, pays the band the ultimate compliment. He calls us "the sound of the fair."

The band is a joy, but it's also a job, and we work at it. This past year we played at the national convention of the Liberal Party of Canada in the Stanley Park Pavilion. Most gratifying, people dancing like mad, some telling us, "We don't have a band like this in…Ottawa, Toronto, wherever…" (Party leader Michael Ignatieff proved to be a pretty good dancer, according to Diane, who'd been watching him.)

*The Dal Richards Orchestra at the PNE in 2009.* Craig Hodge photo

Last year we played tea dances the first Sunday afternoon of each month in the lobby of the Hotel Vancouver. They drew well, but some of the most fun came from seeing the reactions of passengers and crew arriving from the Sunday Air New Zealand flight. They were totally surprised and clearly delighted to hear music in a place where, in other cities, they're just hanging around waiting to check in. And, as always, there were people with stories to tell. Morry and Alanah Hubbermin and son, Ethan, of White Rock, BC, attended the first of the dances, which fell, to the day, on the fiftieth anniversary of their wedding, when the reception was held at the Roof.

Is all this activity tiring? No way. It's too much fun. Would I trade my performing for anything? Not a chance.

# Duets (Finale)

*"Dal has a curiosity about everything. He finds life fascinating. He'll watch the first set at the Jazz Cellar, then excuse himself because he has to go to see the second set at the Orpheum. He's ninety-one and his schedule is incredible. He and Muriel go to see every show they can squeeze in. When we're working he'll turn the band over to Jamie or me so he can jump off the stage and talk to the people and he loves it when they tell him stories of the old days when they saw him at the Roof. He's made this band a family. We watch out for one another, and we all get our moment to shine. It's just an honour to be a part of it."*

Diane Lines, keyboard and vocals.

Muriel has a great line when people ask how we met, which is, of course, a nice way of asking how two people with such an age disparity could ever start dating, let alone marry. "We met in school," she says, "but I took better care of myself."

*My friend, my wife, my right arm—Muriel Honey, on our wedding day, Sept. 7, 2001. I don't know how she does it, juggling both her career and mine, and family too. But she manages beautifully and we still find time for fun.*

So let's get the numbers out of the way, because that's all they are: numbers. Muriel Honey Richards is thirty-one years my junior. We were married four days before 9/11—September 7, 2001—in St. Andrew's-Wesley United Church by the Reverend Gordon Turner (a one-time trombone player from Toronto who introduced the Sunday Jazz Vespers concerts that have become a tradition at the church), but we'd been together about four years before that. She is a successful career woman with two grown daughters, and she probably didn't realize when we got together that she would also become the person who organizes me, handles my office work, makes certain I'm where I'm supposed to be when I'm supposed to be, with the right instrument under my arm, and kids that when I go to my just reward she's going to stuff my pockets with napkins because I'm forever writing notes on them and she wouldn't want me caught short.

And yes, we are in love. That's a given.

I know some people find that unlikely. Seeing their reactions is all part of the fun. Besides, she's right: we did meet in school. She was an eighteen-year-old out of New Westminster Secondary School in her first year of a broadcast communications program at BCIT, I was a fifty-year-old band leader, married to Lorraine, in the second year of my hotel management course.

We must have met or run into each other. There were about thirty people in my course and no more than twenty-two people in hers including, as it turned out, Mike Watt, who played drums in my orchestra and whose father, Pete, was in the Kits band with me. But the earth didn't move.

*Wedding day brunch, Sept. 7, 2001, the first official gathering of Muriel's and my families.*

We were two people at opposite ends of the age spectrum, both getting on with our lives.

Muriel married Rick Honey, who became the afternoon drive personality on radio station CKNW and a sought-after dinner speaker, and raised two daughters, Jennifer and Kayce. Rick and Muriel divorced in 1982. The way we got together years later is the stuff of a TV sitcom.

After a career behind the scenes in radio and public relations, including an intense couple of years as the Vancouver spokesman for Rick Hansen's Man in Motion World Tour, Muriel became a communications and media staffer for Vancouver mayor Gordon Campbell, stayed on with new mayor Philip Owen and became his executive assistant. I think it was some time in 1997 when I joined Hugh Pickett and Norman Young, two of the co-founders of the BC Entertainment Hall of Fame, to see Mayor Owen talk about what was being planned to usher in the new millennium on New Year's Eve 1999. What surprised me was that Muriel, whose name and face I recognized, but whose position in the mayor's office I hadn't known, sat in on the meeting with the mayor. And the first thing I noticed was the greatest pair of legs I'd ever seen in my life.

Apparently she wasn't that impressed. Hugh, Norman and I were all in our mid-80s. When we left, as she later confessed, she looked at the mayor and said: "Now, *there* is optimism. Any one of those guys will be lucky to be *alive* in the new millennium, let alone planning a celebration."

Over the next few years we kept running into each other at various events. Muriel and Hugh often had lunch together, and one day she suggested he bring me along. It sort of developed from there. By that time Muriel had left the mayor's office and rejoined the Rick Hansen Man in Motion organization for his tenth anniversary year. Now she was working on Granville Island, fighting the plans to build a movie theatre there. We'd meet for coffee or lunch, a kind of casual courtship that lasted six to eight months. Muriel's condo, it turned out, was in a building across from mine. When I was on the road she'd condo-sit or come over to water the plants. When I was in town I'd drop over to her place. My own answer when people ask me how we got together is "I borrowed one cup of sugar too many." ("As if he'd know what to *do* with a cup of sugar," she snorts.)

On our first date I took her to dinner. We argued about which side of the street to walk on to get there, each tugging at the other's sleeve. On the way home I revealed a hidden vice: I bought an ice cream cone—the first, she insists, of

*Muriel and me on the grounds of a southern plantation while on a trip to New Orleans in the spring of 2001.*

about ten thousand since we met. Ice cream cones are my thing. I don't have a particular favourite flavour, although if pressed I will vote for rum and raisin.

The thing is, Muriel is every bit as high profile as I am. She currently manages a staff of eight and runs the city's film and special events office, which means she's in charge of coordinating with film producers on such things as street closures for movie shoots, neighbourhood notification when such scenes may lead to temporary inconvenience, and the issuing of permits for scenes involving fires, explosions, car crashes and such. She is nothing if not definite. Once in a while, having heard her deal on the phone with people who do not like her decisions, I

*Cruising is a favourite pastime because it gets us away from phone calls and computers, but we call home for messages at every stop. I wouldn't want to miss a gig request.*

introduce her as "my wife, Muriel, the bitch from City Hall." It gets a laugh from those who know her.

All the age difference has done is teach us to enjoy every moment, which we all should do but most don't. So, when we stroll arm in arm down the street, chances are some heads will turn. In the beginning we'd catch the second looks and exchange a smile.

This reminds me of an incident that took place in London in 1998. I was coming back from a river cruise in Russia, up the Volga from Moscow to St. Petersburg on the motor ship *Lenin* (of course) as a group leader for Canadian tourists and as night time entertainer, playing with Russian musicians who knew all the tunes of Cole Porter, George Gershwin, Johnny Mercer, Irving Berlin, Duke Ellington, et al.

*A stop at the University of Moscow in 1998. Later that day I boarded the Lenin for a ten-day Volga River cruise. I played with a trio of very talented Russian musicians while we sailed from Moscow to St. Petersburg.*

Travel agents had asked whether I'd be interested. Why not? The pay was only $100 a day US, but that was totally in my pocket and other cruises meant a lot of free trips to Alaska, the Caribbean, the Mediterranean, Panama, the Mexican Riviera, Hawaii, Florida, Casablanca (where we went to a bar decorated with paraphernalia and I sang *As Time Goes By*). Great fun.

The Russian ship on the river cruise basically comprised three groups—American, English and Canadian—totalling about four hundred passengers. Every stop we made we would march down the gangplank to shore to be met by busker groups on the wharf—trumpet, trombone, drum, usually an accordion, sometimes a violin. One common denominator was the music, cleverly arranged, with an eye to bigger tips, to be appropriate for the individual groups. The Brits would be greeted by the *Colonel Bogey March*, the Americans would hear *The Star Spangled Banner*, the Canadians, *O, Canada*, all played with open instrument cases hopefully out, US dollars being the currency of the river.

At the first stop where I heard them play *O, Canada*, part of it jarred on my ear—one single note in the second bar, played a halftone lower than it should be. "It's Russia," I shrugged. Close enough. But at the next stop I heard the same thing. Different group, same clinker. So I walked up to the trumpet player and indicated I wanted to look at his music. Sure enough: second bar, a halftone down. The music was a hand-written manuscript, which meant it was probably photocopied and sent all over the country with the mistake in it.

"No, no!" I told the trumpeter, who turned out to be the leader. I pointed to the bar on the music and sang it as it was intended. Recognizing the better sound, his face lit up and he gave me a big bear hug. So all along the river at every stop I did the same thing, my own cultural exchange between Russia and Canada, I figured.

At the end of the cruise we all flew to London to catch the plane back to Vancouver. Very coincidentally, Muriel had flown to Liverpool for three days to supervise a video for a PR client. The plan was, she would catch a train to London and we'd go see a performance of the musical *Chicago*. I'd told the group that my sweetie was coming in, and had taken some ribbing. But something came up, she couldn't make it, and I went to see *Chicago* alone.

*On a trip to Russia, the dockside buskers greeted us with their version of* O Canada, *and were only too happy when I corrected one note of their version. I spoke no Russian, but music is an international language.*

The next day, people in the group were asking me, with sly grins, how things had gone with my sweetie, no doubt thinking "A sweetie? What's this guy gonna do with a sweetie?"

I'm sure some of them weren't sure if I was joking or not when I told them we had to settle for phone sex.

She is a marvel, my wife. Keep in mind that she has a full-time job, then comes home and helps run the business end of mine. And believe me, that's busy. The band business has changed a lot over the years. In the old days negotiations were seat-of-the-pants things and a handshake was as good as a contract. I remember once when a guy put a club on the second floor of the Crown Hotel on Hastings Street across from Woodward's and booked my band for three nights for the opening. I was managing the Devonshire Hotel at the time. He'd come with cash for one night and drop it on my desk. I'd say, "Same time tomorrow?" and he'd come back the next day with some more, all cash.

It used to be "I'll be there for this much. See you." Today, everything is contracted in advance. A stage plot is required, showing how many musicians, what instruments they'll play and where they'll be sitting, as well as a sound plot showing where the microphones and monitors will be, and every gig is different depending on how many musicians are involved. There's the Vancouver Musicians Association contracts, the payroll for the musicians, GST and pension deductions, invoices for everything, promotional material—and whatever it is, everybody wants it *now*. On the rare occasions when Muriel comes with me to a gig she says she's not a roadie, she's more like a Sherpa guide on Mount Everest.

Then there's the web page to update and run, forty to fifty e-mails per day, research for *Dal's Place AM 650* radio shows—add it up and we probably spend twelve to fifteen hours a week at home on the computer, a machine with which I have only a nodding acquaintance.

When we're out at a party or some sort of function we have great fun, but there's no clinging. We separate and work the room, meeting everyone, exchanging stories and gossip. We're both social people who enjoy the music, the conversation, the noise and the laughter. But when we're at home, that's a whole different story.

There's no music. I've got a huge CD collection, of course, but they're never on. Neither is the radio or the TV except for the national news at 11 p.m. and the local news at 11:30. We bought one of those Wii computer consoles with some games—took us a month to set it up and we've probably used it about five minutes' worth. We read a lot in companionable silence, happy in the togetherness. We go to bed at midnight. Muriel gets up at 7 a.m. and heads off to work. Depending on what I've got going for the day, I stay in bed longer.

Having said that, we are out a lot for show openings at the Playhouse and Stanley theatres, attending a couple of Vancouver Symphony Orchestra concerts each month and catching touring shows. Also, as an ambassador-at-large for the Great Canadian Gaming Corporation along with my gigs at the River Rock and Boulevard casinos, I enjoy access to the visiting shows and have made friends with some of the artists we've seen. We love to travel to New York in September to catch the Broadway shows and visit jazz clubs and to chill out in Maui in January. We are both determined to keep fit. Muriel competes in the Sun Run and has a personal trainer. I attend fitness classes at the Roundhouse, swim twenty lengths at the YWCA each Thursday and we can be seen taking long walks through downtown on our way to and from theatres and events.

I guess you could say that I am not overly patient, particularly when circumstances keep me from doing what I want to do. In 2007, when it was apparent that both my knees were beyond Mother Nature's ability to repair, I had one replaced. When the replacement passed medical muster at my six-week checkup I said, "Okay, let's do the other one." The surgeon had a cancellation, so I worked July 9 in Duncan on Vancouver Island, came home the next day, had the surgery July 11, met a commitment to appear at a woman's 100th birthday party a week after surgery and did three big festival gigs two weeks later. I threw myself into the rehabilitation program at the Mary Pack Arthritis Centre, which has a pool, a gym and an exercise machine room. When the instructor asked for twenty repetitions, I'd do forty. I wasn't showing off, I simply had a great incentive. My regular seventeen-day, two-shows-a-day gig at the PNE was coming up in August. I was determined to be on that bandstand. And I was.

At my final post-surgery checkup the surgeon, Dr. Donald Werry, said he'd never had a patient whose recovery was so fast and so complete. It was such good news that I ignored the taxis and walked the mile-plus route home from his office.

Speaking of Beatty Street, allow me to switch gears for a moment. Now would be a good time to make another low bow of gratitude to my father, without whom we might be living who-knows-where. Way back in 1945 when I announced that Beryl and I were getting married, his first piece of advice came in a two-word package: "Don't rent." An interesting thought, since we certainly didn't have the money to buy a house. When I pointed this out, he added two more words: "Build one," he said—another interesting idea because I'd never done any building. My father wasn't taking no for an answer. "You've worked in the machine shop," he said. "You have a lot of savvy with tools. You can do this." We got a piece of property. Then we got a guy with a scoop and a horse to pull it as we set about digging out the basement. It was probably the last house in town with a horse-dug basement. I hired a man with some carpentry experience and my father helped. It took about a year, but between us we built that first house.

Why do I mention that now? Because if I hadn't scraped together the money to build it, if I'd ignored my father's advice and begun our married life in an apartment, I might never have had the equity to buy the next one, and the one after that. And Muriel and I probably wouldn't be sitting in our two-level loft in a hundred-year-old warehouse, surrounded by all the photographs and CDs and books and memorabilia.

The old warehouse building had been converted to thirty-two suites just before Expo '86, and sat there empty because no one was interested. Ahead of its time, I guess. Expo officials leased them for a while, but in 1987 the suites went up for auction. I saw the ad, and decided to take a look.

The smaller suites, some 900 square feet, had an opening bid price of $154,000. The largest, the one I wanted, was 2,500 square feet and opened at $178,000. I sat there, fingers crossed as the auctioneer gave it the going-once-going-twice spiel. But there were no takers. By then I'd read the fine print: purchasers had to deposit a $5,000 certified cheque, but with so little interest expressed by anyone, I thought there might be a way around that. I went up and made my pitch: if I could come up with the money by 10 a.m. the next morning, would they sell me the loft for the minimum? They said yes, and the next morning I had my new apartment.

It's made such great sense for me. The CBC is within walking distance, as are the downtown hotels and clubs and BC Place Stadium. There's a vibrancy to the area. You can *feel* it growing as the city gets ready for the Olympic Games. Over the years it's exceeded my expectations, and now Muriel's office is also but a walk away. The value has skyrocketed, but we're here for the duration.

Muriel laughingly tells people that, if she loses track of me at a party or reception or at one of the many fund-raising dinners we attend regularly, she just looks for the nearest good-looking blonde and usually spots me close by. Just a coincidence, of course. It happened last spring at a reception following a Diana Krall concert at the Orpheum, but this time with a bit of a twist. While Muriel was sitting in a corner of the Orpheum's West Coast Hall chatting with local concert promoter Paul Mercs, she glanced up to find me with what she calls a "fine-figured leggy blonde" with her arm draped over my shoulder. But this time Muriel's attention was caught by the sparkly red shoes that Diana had flashed on stage during the show, a gift from hubby Elvis Costello, and watched with amusement as Diana led me across the room to meet her father.

I should confess: I do like women. Always have, and hopefully always will. For most of those years I've been married, but there were a few years after I lost Lorraine to cancer and before I met Muriel that there were other women in my life. I've never been good at living on my own, never wanted to try.

Wendy Harvey was a colleague at the Variety Club, and several months after Lorraine's death I no longer wanted to remain alone in the home we had lived in, so I moved in with Wendy in her apartment in Kerrisdale. We shared our commitment to the children of Variety and a love of travel, and spent three or four years together travelling to Variety International conventions in London, Australia and Jerusalem. Wendy didn't want to move downtown, I did, and that ended the relationship but not the friendship— we still work together at the Variety Children's Christmas party and lunch regularly, too.

It wasn't long after I moved in to Beatty Street that Marilyn Ployart moved in with me. We'd met years before; she was a big fan of the band, and became a very supportive friend. Marilyn and I lived together for almost ten years; she played an important role in my life for a number of years, but by the late 1990s we had drifted into somewhat

*En route home after a Variety Club international convention in Jerusalem, Aurla Dueck (l), Wendy Harvey and I climbed aboard camels—a trick in itself—for a visit to the Pyramids.*

separate lives; I was out and about at lunches, receptions and events while Marilyn preferred to stick closer to home. It wasn't until I realized that many of the people I'd met during that time didn't even know that Marilyn was part of my life that I understood that we'd grown apart, not together. I was turning eighty, but not ready to stop and smell the roses. I wanted my life to continue to be exciting and busy. And then I met Muriel and, much to my surprise—and hers—we became a couple. It was a difficult few months, but Marilyn and I managed to part on good terms, and we still see each other occasionally. She was and is a dear friend of Juliette's.

All right, I admit it: there's another woman in my life. This one has been, remains and always will be a keeper: my daughter, Dallas Richards Chapple. I'll let her tell you about it. This is her contribution to my ninetieth birthday program.

*To you he is Dal Richards, a man whose many achievements include performing for a record twenty-five years at the Panorama Roof with my mother, Lorraine McAllister, being honoured with both the Order of BC and the Order of Canada and still, at the incredible age of ninety (and I do hope it's genetic!) performing 125 gigs a year. Let me give you a peek behind the curtain at the extraordinary man whom I am proud to call my father.*

*My father is…always there. Whether I've wanted to share my achievements or drown my sorrows, my father has always been there to listen and to talk. We also share a sensibility and love of music and fine performance, as we did last year when we travelled to New York together to see six shows in five days! There is no better tour guide of the nightspots of New York or the history of big band swing than my father.*

*My father is…insatiably curious—the hallmark of a very bright mind. When I was doing graduate work in Communications at the Sorbonne, my dad took a course, too. How many fathers do you know who would audit a Communications course at UBC just so he could understand what his daughter was studying and be able to discuss it with her?*

*My father is…a talented and generous musician. He attends almost every live performance of every artist in town to learn and to experience whatever art, skill and talent they share with audiences. He is also a nurturer of young talent. Whether it is Michael Kaeshammer, Michael Bublé or Bria Skonberg, my father gets excited about helping others achieve success. I believe it's this enthusiasm that keeps him young.*

*Above all, my father is…my best friend. For me there is nothing like a phone call from my dad. We share so many things in common that to talk and laugh with him always makes me happy. All my life I have shared him with others. I know that after reading [the program articles] you will love him as I do.*

Being a band leader's kid is not something out of a *Father Knows Best* script. Daddy wasn't home a lot at nights and when she awoke to go to school in the morning he'd be sleeping. Some of her birthdays were celebrated ringside at the Cave. On one such occasion Mitzi Gaynor came to the edge of the stage, leaned over, looked at her and said, "You look just like me!" On her sixteenth, the man sitting next to her was Oscar Peterson, the Hall of Fame jazz pianist that Duke Ellington once called "the maharaja of the keyboard." As mentioned earlier, Oscar had been with the Johnny Holmes band when Lorraine sang with them in Montreal. On his Canadian tour he picked up local musicians and we accompanied him at the PNE for his show at the Garden Auditorium.

She is one smart cookie, my daughter. Bachelor of Arts degree in English literature from University of BC with an undergrad degree in Communications; two and a half years at the Sorbonne; PhD thesis on The Sociology of Mass Communication at the University of Paris, attending classes at night while working with UNESCO by day.

As a part-time receptionist with the CBC in Vancouver while attending UBC she met her future husband, Len Chapple. They reconnected when she returned to Canada and rejoined the network in the department of strategic planning, and were married in 1981. Len was the CBC's director for the Montreal Olympics in 1976, the Commonwealth Games in Edmonton and the Calgary Olympics for CTV in 1988. They lived in Seattle for two years while he worked for Ted Turner's Goodwill Games, and following another stint with the Commonwealth Games in Victoria they set up residence there, where Dallas has a highly successful career in real estate as an associate with RE/MAX.

Oh, did I mention the six pink Cadillacs? While she was in Toronto she left the CBC and joined Mary Kay cosmetics, running a team of 75 consultants and winning one of their famous pink autos for sales volume. The car was replaced with a new one every two years.

Dallas has a thing about Father's Day. Every year she picks me up and takes me away to do something different, all of them having something to do with transportation. Once we rented a Sea-Doo, tried to get on the same one, and wound up in the ocean. Had to rent two and go solo. Once she took me on a mystery tour by car to Hope, where she'd reserved a glider. Just the two of us and the pilot. When we released from the carrier plane and swooped over the countryside, the silence was awesome.

*Top: Father's Day in Hope, BC.*

*Above: On a trip to Maui in 1972, my daughter Dallas and I tried our hand at scuba lessons. Dallas is forever looking for and finding ways to turn Father's Day celebrations into adventures.*

On other Father's Days there'd be whale watching in a boat off Victoria, a helicopter ride from Grouse Mountain, a trip down the Fraser River by paddlewheeler, kayaking around Butchart Gardens, a seaplane trip to Seattle for lunch…. Once we boarded an amphibious bus at the dock in Victoria. Darn thing went into the water, cruised a bit, then rolled up onto the shore where we were soon ducking trees. It's no longer in service. Don't know what's going to happen next Father's Day. Dallas says she's running out of transportation modes. But I know her. She'll think of something.

Since settling in Victoria, Dallas has served a six-year term on the Victoria Symphony Board of Directors. On one occasion my band went over and teamed up with the symphony string section for a fundraising concert at the Empress Hotel that netted $31,000. It must have been a good show. At one point the band leader jumped off the stage and began to dance with one of the organizers.

So here I am, blessed with two smart chicks: a gorgeous wife at home, and a gorgeous daughter just a phone call away. The gods must have smiled on me.

*New Year's Eve, 2007, with the two women in my life, Muriel and Dallas. Every day, I count my blessings and marvel at my luck.*

# Dal's Place

*"Dal's Place is like your favourite old bedroom slippers. Sure, you could get new ones, but why would you when the old ones are just right?"*

Steve Bush, producer, The Sound Kitchen.

My radio show started innocently enough. CJAZZ had a show called *Sounds of the Big Bands*, produced by Harry Boon. Once in a while I'd drop off a record and occasionally go on the air with the host. The show moved to CHQM-FM, which had a memory music format. Before long, Brian Scharf, the station's director of sales, offered me my own program.

Well, why not? I knew the music, the format pretty much guaranteed that people who wanted to hear the big band sound would know where to tune in, and a weekly show would get the word out on where the band was appearing. The station had used the memory music format for thirty years. Everything looked solid. So there I was, doing a Sunday night hour featuring music of the '40s, '50s and '60s, and enjoying every minute of it. Then, on Chinese New Year's Eve, February 9, 1994, the station played Bob Hope's *Thanks for the Memories* and, after a brief pause, signed on again with an all-night Chinese program, the forerunner to all-Chinese programming seven months later. The show had developed a following—not huge, but loyal and growing. It was picked up by AM1040, a bit of a spit-and-baling-wire operation. I called it *Memory Lane*, which drew an irate call from Jack Cullen, CKNW's legendary late-night jazz and oldies deejay. "My territory," he said.

Fair enough. We ran a listeners' name-the-show contest, a weekend at the Bayshore Hotel for the winning entry. Nobody suggested *Dal's Place* but me, and people might not have approved if I declared myself the winner. So we held a draw from the entries, awarded the prize—and called the show *Dal's Place* anyway, as it's been ever since. It was my show, so I made the rules.

Then AM1040 disappeared from the airwaves, but Jimmy Pattison's station, AM600 made a weekend spot for us, and I struck gold in the form of a musician and techno wizard named Steve Bush, who produced and operated the show with the kind of expertise you'd never get from someone who just knew which buttons to push or switches to throw. I found that out when Steve got an offer from Paul Airey in 2005 to become his principal producer at the Sound Kitchen production house. Working with new operators just wasn't the same. But Steve and Paul rescued me. "How about doing the show over here," they said, "and we deliver the disk to the radio station?"

Perfect. It's been that way ever since. Even the move to AM650 when Jimmy got his FM licence and AM600 ceased to exist was seamless. Much of AM650's programming was

*Thanks to Steve Bush at the Sound Kitchen, I always know the production of* Dal's Place *will be first class—and a whole lot of fun doing the research and swapping stories with the guests.* Steve Bush photo

similar to AM600's, and I just kept going to the Sound Kitchen to record it. I am so indebted to Paul and to Steve, whose production skills and understanding of me, the music and the show make it a fun process, especially when you consider that the Sound Kitchen has an entranceway built like a '50s café with a booth, stools, counter and even those old-fashioned counter-top juke boxes. Cookies are often available—and ice cream! Thanks to Paul's wife, Judy, there's always a jar of candies on the counter. Eat your heart out, CBC.

It's a wonderful partnership. Because he's a musician as well as a technician. Steve can take a song that would run too long, lift the second saxophone solo out of it with the integrity of the song first and foremost in his mind, and the listeners will never know. Because we pre-tape, if I stumble or screw up and don't catch it myself, we have such an understanding and mutual trust that he can laugh and say, "Well, that sucked. Let's try it again." You can see why I asked Steve to produce my latest CD, *Dal Richards and Friends: One More Time!*

People ask me what I get out of doing the show. It's simple: I enjoy the music, the guests, and the research and writing that goes into the scripts. I know a lot of the background of the songs and the bands and singers on them, but I'll research, say, Anita O'Day, looking for some bits of information that the listening audience isn't likely to know and would enjoy discovering. I'll see a single sentence in an article and think, "Oh, that's a story. That will hook up with..." It's like mining: look hard enough and who knows what nuggets you'll find?

Having the week's in-studio guest bring three or four personal favourite songs gives us conversational flexibility. I know in advance what the songs will be, which allows me to flesh out the performance, and the guests usually have stories of why the song was selected and what it's meant to them. VSO maestro Bramwell Tovey, jazz guitarist John Pizzarilli, Boston Pops conductor Keith Lockhart, radio and TV personality Vicki Gabereau, Vancouver historian Chuck Davis, BC Lions president Bob Ackles, a huge fan of jazz, *Hot Air* jazz show host Paul Grant—everyone has a story. Doc Severinsen had tales of his days as band leader on the Johnny Carson show. Pete Fountain painted the New Orleans jazz scene. Anne Murray, whom I interviewed before her live show at the Boulevard Casino, offered an insight when she apologized and said she had to go and exercise her vocal chords for fifteen minutes before the show. "They're muscles," she explained. "You have to keep them in shape."

*Muriel and I attend the Vancouver Symphony Orchestra concerts regularly, and support the VSO through annual donations. VSO Musical Director Bramwell Tovey poses with me under my BC Entertainment Hall of Fame photo in the Orpheum's upper lobby.* Dave Roels photo

After playing a few tunes selected by my guest, I have The Question.

Let's say, for example, the guest is a well-known singer who's in town for a gig at the Queen Elizabeth Theatre. I say something like "Assume for a moment that your performance is such a sensation that management decides to give you a special reward: For one night only, you get to bring your friends, fill the Stanley Theatre and hear a show featuring all of your all-time favourites, living or dead. Sinatra, Ella, the Ellington band, your favourite original cast Broadway show. The choices are yours.

"Now, here's the question: Whom do you choose? Don't forget—anyone, any era, living or dead."

At the very least it triggers discussion, and sometimes the answers are startling. *Vancouver Sun* theatre critic Peter Birney picked a bunch of old-time radio comedians: Jack Benny, Fred Allen, Bob Hope, Sid Caesar, Wayne and Shuster. Bob Blackwood, who writes the liner notes for my CDs, wanted to be seated in New York's Aeolian Hall among the audience there on February 12, 1924, to hear the debut performance of George Gershwin's *Rhapsody in Blue* by the Paul Whiteman orchestra, with Gershwin himself as the featured pianist. You just never know, and that's the charm of it.

I've done a lot of other radio over the years. In 1944, when the CBC launched the Dominion Network, a cross-Canada linking of independent stations, and named CJOR as its Vancouver affiliate, one of the shows produced here—across the street from CJOR's studio in the Grosvenor Hotel in a vacant store rather grandly called a theatre—was called

*Long-time friend Bob Blackwood, who writes the liner notes for my CDs, was also the master of ceremonies for my eightieth birthday party at the Panorama Roof in 1998.* Dave Roels photo

*After Dark*, late-night music featuring the Dal Richards Sextet with Beryl and me on vocals, originating here at 8:30 p.m. and, given the three-hour time difference, closing network broadcasting in the east. Hence, the name.

In 1988, the CBC's *Arts National* radio show host, Ian Alexander, asked me if, given complete access to station record and music libraries across the country, I could write and narrate a series of hour-long programs featuring Canadian bands of the past fifty years. *Arts National* had been a Friday night CBC fixture for years with Canadian history and content. I happily agreed. Between the material in all those libraries and my personal collection I was sure we could cover most of the bands. We did the first five shows from Vancouver and the last of the six out of Toronto in mid-December. The response was so good that they asked if I had any ideas about how to continue it.

*It's duelling trumpets at the 2007 Pattison Group Christmas party, as Jimmy takes a break from hosting to play a tune with Diane, Bria, Ron Thompson and me.*

"British bands during the war years would make for some great stories," I said. We did that one. They wanted more, so we did six more hours featuring the top American bands. It was great fun, great music, and I was *paid* to do it.

I still appear on *Hot Air* perhaps once a year for a jazz discussion, and on the CBC's *Early Edition* morning show with Rick Cluff every Remembrance Day and prior to New Year's Eve. But *Dal's Place* is special to me because I've done it for a long time and know from what people tell me at band appearances how much they enjoy it. The show also makes me a part of the media—minus the fedora with the press card sticking out of the hat band—which means comp tickets to a lot of shows, and gets our band's name out there to people who might not otherwise know of us. So it's all good, as I know our music always will be.

*How do I count the memories from those wonderful nights at the Panorama Roof? One way is to go back through the photos like this one with Lorraine and announcer Stan Peters in 1960.* F.J. Talbot photo

# Encore!

*"Ella Fitzgerald said, 'Don't give up trying what you want to do. Where there's love and inspiration, I don't think you can go wrong.' That's Dal. It's what's propelled him and kept him young. He's the secret. He's got amazing musicians and the music is always good, but it's his spirit. He reaches out and relates to the audience, and to the band. People pick up on the energy. I look at him and I think 'That's the kind of person I want to strive to be.'"*

Jennifer Hayes, vocalist.

I've never been much for looking back. Too curious about what lies ahead, I suppose—the songs still to be played, the PNE shows yet to do, the New Year's Eve dances that never get old, the rush that still comes when the applause rolls over you like a wave of thank-yous and no matter how many times you've heard it on how many stages or bandstands it's always fresh and new.

It took a lot of convincing before I'd do a book. Jim Taylor bugged me for several years. "You're the last of your kind, the last one who lived and played in the '30s, '40s and '50s," he kept saying. "When you die, all the stories die with you. We can't let that happen."

I thought about that for a long time. Finally, I phoned him. "Okay, Jim," I said. "Let's do it. When do you want to start?"

"You're ninety years old," he said. "How about yesterday?"

He gave me a digital recorder ("One button," Muriel warned him.) The plan was that whenever I thought of a story that might be good for the book I'd turn it on and put in a reminder to tell him about the so-and-so. I went him one better. I set up meetings with dozens of old cronies in the music and hotel business, the PNE, radio and TV, Variety, family, friends, relatives etc. Over lunch or coffee we swapped remembrances that brought back long-forgotten names and tales of the Vancouver music scene when it was young and just beginning to show all its talent-rich promise.

One question I got over and over again when I said we were writing a book was "Why him? The guy's a sports writer." But I'd been in Jim's basement sorting through his hundreds of old LPs. He knew and loved the music. He'd appeared several times on *Dal's Place*. Besides, how could I not go with a guy who, at seventeen and a jazz fan even then, wrote a record column for Victoria's *Daily Colonist* in which he plugged the new release *Tea for Two Cha-Cha* by Warren Covington and the new Tommy Dorsey Orchestra, sneered at Elvis Presley's *Heartbreak Hotel* and assured readers that "within six months to a year the name Presley will bring forth, instead of screams of delight, one comment: 'Who?'"

In 2006 the Downtown Vancouver Business Improvement Association had a series of mosaics reflecting the city's history installed on downtown streets. The Fairmont Hotel Vancouver sponsored mine, located outside their Georgia entrance. Hotel manager Mark Andrews gets a blast of thanks from me for doing so. Dave Roels photo

It's funny how the process has worked. Little snippets of memory have popped up at unexpected moments, each triggering another. I remember Mel and Dorothy at home with the folks, and the games of Monopoly and bridge, then bounce to the time, five or six years after I left Magee, when the then-leader of the school band asked me to come and listen and offer opinions on their progress—and there, playing tenor sax, sat my brother, Mel. I didn't even know he was *in* the band, let alone playing saxophone. From there the memory ricochets to Mel's career, how he joined the Air Force at seventeen, returned after service to complete high school, went to UBC and majored in soil science, then went into teacher training, spent his career in education and retired as principal of Steveston Senior Secondary School. Many of the people who come to say hello to me after a gig tell me what a great teacher Mel was—it makes me proud. My sister, Dorothy, comes into the memory picture as well, she who lost her fiancé in the war and never married, and had a successful career in the Bank of Toronto's head office in Vancouver.

But mostly, and I guess it's understandable, my memories are of the music and my life in it, the people and the places who've made it such an adventure. It's all been great fun, and still is.

With corporate events, weddings, anniversaries, birthdays and the occasional grand opening, the band is still busy. In May this year we recorded *Dal Richards and Friends, One More Time*, in the CBC's renovated Studio One. What an honour it was to be chosen as the first band to record using the latest technological marvel, and to

*Unveiling my BC Entertainment Hall of Fame plaque in front of the Orpheum on Granville Street following my induction in 1994.*

work with John Mang, Manager, Production and Resources, CBC Radio, BC; Richard Champagne, recording supervisor and lead engineer; and crew Don Harderm, Gary Heald, Chris Cutress and Bruce Diedrich. The CBC also distributed the CD to its stations across Canada, which assured us of the kind of exposure you need as a launching pad in the ultra-competitive recording industry. I look ahead and anticipate big things for the band, and if ever a talented bunch of musicians deserved big things, it is this one. As for me personally, I've been in training with Muriel not just to stay fit but to prepare myself to fulfill another dream: I want to be one of the torchbearers for the 2010 Winter Olympic Games. Dreams have played a huge part in my life. If you don't have them, if you don't dare to push yourself, then you rob yourself of targets and the joy that comes when you achieve them.

The proof is in the generations of people who've danced to my bands and come to the bandstand with stories of the times they first danced to them, decades before. Often, as I gaze out over the dance floor while the band does *In the*

*Recording our latest CD, Dal Richards and Friends, One More Time! at the CBC's recently renovated Studio One. A long, long way from the single stand-up microphone.* Chris Cutress photo

*Mood* or *Stardust* or *As Time Goes By*, I can see two, even three generations sharing the floor and the music.

As for the teenagers, you'd think they'd be a tough sell because with them it has to be a happening, not so much listening to a show as being a *part* of a total experience. They're not of a generation that sits and listens. Yet, I've seen it happen time and again when we're playing the open air concerts at the PNE. The kids walk through the grounds with determined strides, heading for the midway, but to get there they have to pass the outdoor bandstand. It's not their music, but pretty soon they stop, listen for a few seconds, some of them sit down, and before you know it they're caught up in the music.

Other young people make it a point to come to the show, and to come up to talk to me. When I ask how they got interested in the music, they tell me their dad or grandfather had the records. Many have played in school bands. They know who Cole Porter was as opposed to Irving Berlin. They know about Goodman and Miller and Dorsey, and they want to know more. People ask me how I stay so young. Simple. It's the music and the people of all ages who love to hear it.

They bring back memories, those kids. I look at them and I see Jack Bensted and me, hunched over the radio late at night in 1935 listening to Benny Goodman live from New York. The hour didn't matter, only the music. Now it's the same with them.

It's been an amazing, wonderful ride, and now there seems a new level to it, a career encore—an oeuvre, the French call it, a recognition of my life's work and career. I

*Receiving an honorary doctorate from BC Institute of Technology, 1999. Of the many career decisions over the years, the one to enroll in BCIT's hotel management course was at the top of the list.*

think it surfaced on my ninetieth birthday, and it seems to be growing. Last June, for example, at a city-wide sold-out Friday afternoon seniors' tea dance, the guests wanted to talk to me, to have their pictures taken with me. Some just wanted to touch me, which I found very sweet. (I'm sure Michael Bublé and Bryan Adams are used to that sort of thing, but for a ninety-one-year-old it's a real high. I turned the band over to Jamie while I wandered through the crowd and spoke to them, which they seemed to appreciate.) At a Variety club dinner at the River Rock Casino that featured a series of speakers, most seemingly felt compelled to mention my name. My advanced age, I've discovered, has its merits, and it leaves me humbly grateful. Holding a fundraiser? Get Dal Richards. His name will sell tickets. I go to a Board of Trade meeting and the chairman says: "Dal Richards is with us today. Take a bow, Dal." Larry O'Brien brings the current edition of the Glenn Miller Orchestra to town and gives me a plug from the stage for "keeping big band music alive in Vancouver." I've been honoured with both the Order of Canada and the Order of BC. Then-mayor Larry Campbell presented me with the Freedom of the City, including lifetime free parking, free admission to civic facilities and free burial. Who knows how many people have sat or will sit on my bench on the PNE grounds? It brings to mind one of the sayings I pass along to the crowds during shows: "Never regret growing old, for it is a privilege denied to many."

My band has played a part in the opening ceremonies of so many Vancouver landmarks—the Vogue Theatre, Pacific Coliseum, the Queen Elizabeth Theatre, the Pacific Centre, and the Vancouver Art Gallery. We've played at wedding receptions for dear friends like Tania Miller, conductor of the Victoria Symphony, with whom we did concerts when she was assistant conductor of the Vancouver Symphony, and I had the pleasure of the second dance with the bride as she began her life with her husband, Dr. Tom Noonan. We've played at the biggest wedding in Vancouver history: William F. Buckley Jr. and Patricia Taylor in 1950—he the renowned and controversial American journalist, she the daughter of industrialist Austin Taylor, reputed to be the wealthiest man in Vancouver—and at the wedding of Austin Taylor Jr.'s daughter. We can feel we've been a part of the city's growth and history, and take pride in it.

*It was Vancouver's society wedding of the year back in 1950 when American journalist William F. Buckley Jr. wed Patricia Taylor, daughter of Vancouver industrialist Austin Taylor—and my band got the gig at the Taylors' Shannon Estate.* News Herald *photo*

We've had the privilege of working with young musicians in organizations like the West Vancouver Community Band, conducted by Doug Macaulay, whose ninety-six members joined my band on stage at the West Vancouver Ice Arena to play such standards as *In the Mood*, *T.D.'s Boogie Woogie* and *Sing, Sing, Sing*, in which seven drummers joined Gary Mussatto for a rendition that brought down the house.

Quit? No, I couldn't handle that. Retirement is not an option. Besides, it would fly in the face of medical advice. "Don't stop blowing your horn, Dal," my doctor says. "You may drop dead."

*Governor-General Romeo LeBlanc presented me with the Order of Canada in Ottawa in 1994. My folks would be so proud, as am I.*

*Receiving the Order of BC from Lieutenant-Governor Iona Campagnolo, 2003.*

One day the true *Hour of Parting* will come. When it does, I hope I've got a front-row seat in the real Balcony and the bands who've gone before are swinging. Until then, keep your dancing shoes polished and your partner close by. The Dal Richards Orchestra could be coming to a hall near you.

So many walks onstage, so many band members, so many vocalists. So many venues including the Queen Elizabeth Theatre, which Lorraine and the band helped open in 1959. What a life it's been.

# Honours and Awards

Variety Club of BC Heart Award 1992

Canadian 125 Medal 1992

Variety Club International Presidential Citation 1993

Order of Canada 1994

BC Entertainment Hall of Fame Inductee 1994

BCIT Honorary Doctor of Technology 1999

BC Open University Honorary Doctorate 2001

Spirit of Vancouver Inaugural Award 2002

Queen Elizabeth Golden Jubilee Medal 2002

Order of British Columbia 2003

Vancouver Board of Trade Honorary Life Membership
2003

Hugh B. Main Lifetime Achievement Award,
Tourism Vancouver, 2003

Freedom of the City of Vancouver 2005

Honorary Diploma of Music
Vancouver Community College 2005

Western Canadian Music Association Heritage Award
2005

BC Lions Wall of Fame Inductee 2005

Downtown Vancouver Business Association,
Art Jones Lifetime Achievement Award, 2007

PNE President's Lifetime Achievement Award 2007

Vancouver AM Wake Up Award Chairman Emeritus 2007

Honorary Director Sam Sullivan
Disability Foundation 2008

# Index